Easter

Proclamation 3

Aids for Interpreting
the Lessons of the Church Year

Easter

Edgar Krentz

Elizabeth Achtemeier, series editor

Series B

FORTRESS PRESS   Philadelphia

COPYRIGHT © 1985 BY FORTRESS PRESS

Library of Congress Cataloging in Publication Data

Main entry under title:
Proclamation 3.

Consists of 28 volumes in 3 series designated A, B, and C which correspond to the cycles of the three year lectionary. Each series contains 8 basic volumes with the following titles: Advent-Christmas, Epiphany, Lent, Holy Week, Easter, Pentecost 1, Pentecost 2, and Pentecost 3.
1. Bible—Homiletical use. 2. Bible—Liturgical lessons, English. I. Achtemeier, Elizabeth Rice, 1926–
BS534.5.P765   1985   251   84–18756
ISBN 0–8006–4106–X (Series B, Pentecost 1)

1260H84   Printed in the United States of America   1–4105

Contents

Series Foreword

Proclamation 3 is an entirely new aid for preaching from the three-year ecumenical lectionary. In outward appearance this new series is similar to *Proclamation: Aids for Interpreting the Lessons of the Church Year* and *Proclamation 2*. But *Proclamation 3* has a new content as well as a new purpose.

First, there is only one author for each of the twenty-eight volumes of *Proclamation 3*. This means that each author handles both the exegesis and the exposition of the stated texts, thus eliminating the possibility of disparity between scholarly apprehension and homiletical application of the appointed lessons. While every effort was made in *Proclamation: Aids* and in *Proclamation 2* to avoid such disparity, it tended to creep in occasionally. *Proclamation 3* corrects that tendency.

Second, *Proclamation 3* is directed primarily at homiletical interpretation of the stated lessons. We have again assembled the finest biblical scholars and preachers available to write for the series; now, however, they bring their skills to us not primarily as exegetes, but as interpreters of the Word of God. Exegetical material is still presented—sometimes at length—but, most important, here it is also applied; the texts are interpreted and expounded homiletically for the church and society of our day. In this new series scholars become preachers. They no longer stand back from the biblical text and just discuss it objectively. They engage it—as the Word of God for the worshiping community. The reader therefore will not find here the divisions between "exegesis" and "homiletical interpretation" that were marked off in the two earlier series. In *Proclamation 3* the work of the pulpit is the context and goal of all that is written.

There is still some slight diversity between the several lections and calendars of the various denominations. In an effort to overcome such diversity, the North American Committee on a Common Lectionary issued an experimental "consensus lectionary" *(The Common Lectionary)*, which is now being tried out in some congregations and which will be further altered at the end of a three-year period. When the final form of that lectionary appears, *Proclamation* will take account of it. In the meantime, *Proclamation 3* deals with those texts that year that are used by *most* denominations on any given Sunday. It also continues to use the Lutheran numbering of the Sundays "after Pentecost." But Episcopalians and Roman Catholics will find most of their stated propers dealt with under this numbering.

Each author writes on three lessons for each Sunday, but no one method of combining the appointed lessons has been imposed upon the writers. The texts are sometimes treated separately, sometimes together—according to the author's own understanding of the texts' relationships and messages. The authors interpret the appointed texts as these texts have spoken to them.

Dr. Edgar Krentz is Professor of New Testament at the Lutheran School of Theology, Chicago, Illinois. Educated at Concordia Seminary and Washington University in St. Louis, he is widely known as a stimulating lecturer, scholar, archaeologist, bibliographer, and author. Among his books are *The Historical-Critical Method* and a volume in the *Proclamation* 2 series.

The Resurrection of Our Lord
Easter Day

Lutheran	Roman Catholic	Episcopal	Pres/UCC/Chr	Meth/COCU
Isa. 25:6–9	Acts 10:34, 37–43	Acts 10:34–43 or Isa. 25:6–9	Isa. 25:6–9	Isa. 25:6–9 or Acts 10:34–48
1 Cor. 15:19–28	Col. 3:1–4 or 1 Cor. 5:6–8	Col. 3:1–4 or Acts 10:34–43	1 Pet. 1:3–9	1 Cor. 15:19–28 or Col. 3:1–4
Mark 16:1–8 or John 20:1–9 (10–18)	John 20:1–9	Mark 16:1–8	Mark 16:1–8	John 20:1–18 or Mark 16:1–8

Easter tempts the preacher to easy sentimentalism, the observance of a "spring recognition rite" that delights in the reappearance of tulips and the greening of trees. It invites treating the resurrection simply like a happy ending to an otherwise gloomy tale. The lessons for the Easter observance in Series B prevent such facile preaching by calling for a proclamation that unfolds the essence of the resurrection of Jesus and its meaning for today in terms that are partly apocalyptic (lessons 1 and 2) and partly challengingly enigmatic (Gospel). They demand, when read together, consideration of the significance of Jesus' resurrection in realistic, unsentimental fashion.

FIRST LESSON

Isa. 25:6–9 is part of the third major section of I Isaiah, a section describing the judgment of the world and the salvation of Israel (Isaiah, 24—27). Chaps. 1—12 of Isaiah speak of the judgment of Judah and the hope of the messianic king in the face of the impending Syro-Ephraimitic War; it concludes with songs of praise (12:1–6). This is followed by a series of oracles spoken against foreign nations which have oppressed Judah. The oppressors will be laid waste and destroyed (Isaiah, 13—23).

The first lesson comes from the so-called Isaiah Apocalypse (Isaiah 24—27), a section characterized by its description of radical universal judgment and salvation, that reaches even to the heavenly, cosmic powers (24:21–23a). The prophet looks past the present and its evils to

9

the ultimate act of divine judgment and vindication in the future. While chaps. 13—23 dealt with specific peoples and their judgment, this section goes far beyond such limits. It is that which justifies the term "apocalypse," though elements of the genre usually called apocalyptic are missing. There is no animal or numerical symbolism, no use of visions or such special revelations, no cosmic dualism.

Isa. 24:1–20 is a dark, foreboding section that describes the grim devastation that the Lord will bring on all the earth. None will escape: people, priest, slave, master, mistress, maid, buyer, seller (24:1–3). The whole earth will be laid waste and put under a curse (24:3–6) that makes a celebration impossible. The prophet cannot even join in the praise of those who see the hand of the Lord in all this (24:14–16). All is destruction. The judgment of God is fearful. Music is stilled, wine no longer made. Human defenses are shattered: houses are locked against their owners (24:10) and city gates no longer protect (24:12). Cosmic convulsions shake the earth from top to bottom (24:17–20).

Such acts are, however, the process by which the Lord is enthroned as King on Mt. Zion in Jerusalem (24:21–23). All opposing powers are judged: kings are imprisoned (24:21–22); the heavenly bodies, thought of as powers divine (cf. 2 Kings 17:16, Mark 13:24f.; 15:33), are conquered (cf. Isa. 60:19). God, the Righteous (24:16), rules enthroned in Jerusalem; his glory is manifested. Glory is what shows that God is indeed God (cf. Exod. 24:9–11, 16–17; 40:34–38). It is the symbol of his presence among Israel as her God.

Isa. 25:1–5 is a psalm of thanksgiving that praises the Lord for destroying the city in defense of the poor. His glory is revealed in such a defense. Oppressive rulers are cast down. The lesson for Easter follows. Isa. 25:6–8 is an oracle announcing the continuation of 24:21–23. God the King hosts a coronation banquet. That banquet is "for all peoples," a universal celebration that correlates with the universal dominion of the Lord. The picture of the feast is often used to describe the ideal future: Isa. 55:1–2 summons people to a victory banquet, while 65:11–15 uses it as a picture to describe God's saving of his own. Adonijah tried to claim the succession to David by a feast (1 Kings 1:9, 25). The picture is used also in Ps. 23:5; Luke 14:15–24; Matt. 8:11–12. The joy of the banquet is underscored by the double reference to wine and to the eating of rich meat.

Vv. 7–8 shift the picture. The great enemy of humankind will be defeated, death himself. The presence of the King means the removal of the veil from the head, presumably a sign of mourning in the presence of death. The destruction of death is the basis for the removal of the veil and the turning of sorrow into joy. The curse of Gen. 3:3, 19 is reversed. The passage is almost unique in this view of death's defeat in the Old Testament, but finds its continuation in 1 Cor. 15:26 and Rev. 20:14; 21:3–4. There is no mention of resurrection, no suggestion that the dead are given up by death. Rather the stress is on the joy in the victory of God the King, whose rule means the removal of the reproach of his people (Isa. 25:8). It remains for the New Testament to expand this vision into a universal hope for resurrection.

Isa. 25:9 (like 25:1–5) is a hymnic response (as the first person plural makes clear). "On that day" makes clear the tie to vv. 6–8. The hymn stresses that Israel's role in all this was to wait on God's action. Isaiah does not propose a program by which Israel may aid in the establishment of God's rule. Fidelity under oppression is what is needed—and it will turn into joy.

The value of this text for proclamation resides in its very inchoate sense. People still wait on God's action; we are inclined to try to do God's deeds for him. Isaiah reminds us that waiting can itself be a positive thing when forces too great for us to deal with surround and oppress us.

SECOND LESSON

1 Cor. 15:19–28 is the New Testament counterpart to the Isaiah text. Many of the same motifs appear: the setting aside of the enemy death, the rule of God over all opposing forces, the waiting for the future realization. But Paul has also drastically reinterpreted the whole christologically. The reason for the reinterpretation lies in the Corinthian (mis)understanding of Paul's fundamental message. Baptism is a participation in the death of Jesus (Rom. 6:4). The Corinthians understood that to mean that after baptism they lived on the level of the Spirit and were set free from the body. Thus their view that there is "no resurrection of dead people" (1 Cor. 15:12) is fundamentally equivalent to the view that the "resurrection has already taken place," as Hymenaeus and Philetas affirm according to 2 Tim. 2:17–18. Such a view led the Corinthians to rampant individualism (1 Cor. 11:28; 8:9) and self-confident security (10:1–13). Paul is contending a false theology of resurrection.

He begins by arguing that the resurrection of Jesus (though not of all Christians) is a part of the general apostolic proclamation (15:3–5, 11). That kerygma is accepted and confessed by the Corinthians. Yet they do not expect a resurrection to come. Paul argues from the common acceptance of the creed of 15:3–5 that their position contradicts their confession (15:12–19). He concludes that if there is no resurrection, then our tie to Jesus can only be a tie to his death (cf. 2 Cor. 4:10), and Christians are the most unfortunate of people.

But the actuality is far from that. The "but" that introduces v. 20 is the statement of the real condition of things after a summation of the unreal. Christ's resurrection sets a process under way. He is himself the "first fruits of those fallen asleep" (15:20). The phrase may be an allusion to the offering of the first sheaf of the harvest on the day after the Sabbath after Passover, that is, the day on which Jesus was raised. Lev. 23:10–11 describes the offering in the context of Passover. The Jewish philosopher Philo, an older contemporary of Paul's, calls this offering the "first fruits" (*De specialibus legibus* 2.162). The "first fruits" are the first installment of a crop, whose harvest is sure to follow. (Rom. 8:23 uses the term in similar fashion.)

Vv. 21–22 interpret the meaning in terms of Christ's correspondence to Adam. The man Adam activated death in the world (cf. Rom. 5:12); in contrast, Christ activates life in the world. (He is called *pneuma zoopoioun,* a "life-producing Spirit," in 15:45.) It is important that he be a human being, since thus he is the counterfigure to Adam. The future tense in v. 22 ("shall be made alive") is very important, as it is in Rom. 6:5. Christ stands at the head of a new creation, as Adam stood at the head of the old one. (Paul returns to this Adam typology in 15:45–49.)

The significance of the future tense is made clear in the apocalyptic schema Paul unfolds in 15:23–28. Resurrection is a future concept, a hope, for the Christian, not a present possession. Events unroll in proper sequence. Christ is raised as "first fruits"; Christians are raised at his Parousia (cf. 1 Thess. 4:15–17). Parousia is a royal term; it is the technical term for the arrival of a king or his official emissary. The term was used of the arrival of Demetrius Poliorketes in Athens, for example. But the Parousia of Jesus also means the "end" of history (15:24), when God will be enthroned as King because his enemies have been overthrown. Then Jesus will "hand over the royal rule to God the Father" (or "the God and Father"). The title is that used of God as the one who raised Jesus from the dead! (Cf. Gal. 1:4; 1 Thess. 1:9–10; Rom. 10:9; 15:6; 2 Cor. 1:3.) By raising Jesus from the dead God showed he is the powerful creator who can call nonexistent things into being (Rom. 4:17–25 is the major commentary on the phrase). Jesus turns over the rule to God, the King of the universe, because all the powers ("every rule and every authority and power," 15:24; cf. Col. 1:16) will have been set aside, including the last enemy of all, death (15:26). If death were set aside, then the end would be here, for Christ "must rule until God puts all his enemies under his (that is, Christ's) feet." The citation of Ps. 110:1 in v. 25 supports the idea that Christ's resurrection was also his elevation to rule (cf. Rom. 8:34, Heb. 1:3)—and his subservience to God, who raised him from the dead. The last two verses of the passage make that clear by a *gezerah shawah,* a rabbinical mode of interpretation in which passages which use the same term(s) can be brought together. Ps. 8:6 shows that God is not subject to Christ, but Christ to God, who is to be "all in all" (cf. 1 Cor. 8:6; Rom. 11:36).

1 Corinthians is a warning against false complacency in the Christian community. The resurrection of Jesus puts Christians on the way, not at the goal. Luther said of Jesus' resurrection that "it is not enough to know the history; rather we must also know the use and fruit that he gained by the resurrection" (*WA* XVII, I, 86ff.). The second lesson focuses the message of the first by calling attention to the reality of this fruit while we wait.

GOSPEL

Mark 16:1-8, the classical Easter Gospel, is enigmatic at first reading; it underplays what could be a glorious conclusion, in the manner of Matthew or Luke. It is at first even more strange when read in conjunction with the first two lessons for Easter, both of which stress the rule of God and the defeat of the hostile powers. Mark ends at 16:8 with the words "for they were afraid." There is no resurrection appearance, no confession of faith such as Thomas makes in John 20. The attentive reader is left with a curious sense of letdown, of anticlimax. There is no happy ending.

That reading misses what Mark's narrative is all about, because it proceeds from Matthew and Luke with their resurrection appearances and assumes that anything less than that or other than that is inadequate. But the careful reading of Mark suggests something different. The facts of 16:1-8 are clear and familiar. We can rehearse them very quickly. Three women come early to Jesus' tomb, having purchased spices the evening before to embalm the body. Their worry about the large stone covering the door is useless, for the stone is rolled back when they arrive. (There is no statement as to who rolled it away as there is in Matthew. Nor are there apocalyptic signs to accompany it, such as the earthquake in Matt. 28:2.) A young man dressed in white is seated on the right; as 2 Macc. 3:26, 33 show, he is a heavenly messenger. The white clothing supports the identification (cf. Mark 9:3; Dan. 7:9). His sudden appearance scares them and so his initial greeting reassures them. (The term for amazement in v. 5 is not the same as that in v. 8!) He then gives his message (discussed below). They leave, full of trembling and ecstasy, without making any response to the messenger. As they go, they speak to no one, since they "were afraid."

What is remarkable in all this is (1) the description of Jesus as "of Nazareth, who was crucified" in v. 6. It is better translated "Jesus, the Nazarene, the crucified one." Both modifiers are "insult terms." The demons of Mark 1:24 had called him "the Nazarene" in an attempt to gain control over him; Acts 4:10 shows that the reference was an insult. Coupled with "the crucified" it describes Jesus as crude, unlettered, small-town, rejected, and humiliated with a criminal's death (cf. 1 Cor. 1:23, Gal. 3:13 for the evaluation). The one resurrected is described with terms of opprobrium. In the background there shimmers the course of the Gospel, in which Jesus was misunderstood (8:17), opposed (2:1–28), rejected (6:1–6), condemned, and executed.

(2) His resurrection is announced by the heavenly messenger. The resurrected one is the rejected and crucified. That correlates completely with the Markan passion predictions (8:31; 9:31; 10:33, 34). The common name for them conceals the fact that each is also a resurrection prediction. It is precisely his rejection that leads to resurrection. There is no other path to vindication. Mark reports no effort on the part of the women to verify the announcement (though the messenger invites them to look). The message itself, with its recall of the movement of the Gospel, is simply sufficient.

(3) The command in 16:7 recalls yet another motif earlier in the Gospel. The disciples are to go to Galilee; "there you shall see him." Twice the verb "see" is used in the future tense, both times in "Son of man" sayings. Mark 13:24–26 recalls the apocalyptic expectation of the heavenly powers being defeated (cf. Isa. 13:10; 34:4). Then "they will see the Son of man going [not "coming," as it is usually translated] in clouds with great glory." There is an implicit reference to Dan. 7:13–14, the scene which portrays the enthronement of the Son of man. The Markan Apocalypse culminates in the enthronement of the Son of man. That is also what Jesus announces to the Jewish court in response to the question of the High Priest: "I am, and you shall see the Son of man seated on the right hand of power (cf. Ps. 110:1) and going [once again, not "coming"] with the clouds of heaven" (14:62). The heavenly messenger announces that his death has been followed

by enthronement. Jesus is now the exalted Son of man, the viceregent of the universe. As such, there is no place in the Gospel for resurrection appearances. In Galilee, the place of teaching and revelation throughout the Gospel, his disciples will realize his exalted status and lordship.

(4) Light is shed on 16:8. The parallelism between the two parts of the verse ("they went out and fled" parallels "they said nothing to anyone," and "trembling and astonishment had come upon them" parallels "for they were afraid") illuminates the conclusion. The women are so impressed with the revelation of the new status of Jesus that religious awe and ecstasy dominate them. They rush to carry out their commission to tell the disciples because they are under the impress of awe and ecstasy. It is not fright, but the consciousness of Jesus' new status that dominates. The last words of the book underscore Jesus' entirely new role.

These four insights help us to understand the message of Easter for the Markan community and suggest the mode of appropriation for today. Mark's Gospel is written during the Jewish-Roman War of A.D. 66–70 (73). It is written to a community that had recently experienced the irrational persecution under Nero in A.D. 64. The brief account in Tacitus is grim: Nero made up scapegoats (for the great fire): he "punished" the depraved Christians with every punishment. Faced with identification with the Jewish rebels (as a Jewish sect) the Roman church was tempted to a form of Epicurean action: "Escape notice as you live." One might save one's life by a dampened Christian confession and life style. The battered Christian community licked its emotional wounds and was quiet. The Gospel of Mark is a call to confession. "Whoever loses his life for my sake *and the gospel's* (the words are unique to Mark) will save it" (8:35; cf. 8:38). Mark 10:29–31 stress the same action "for my sake and *for the gospel*." Mark 13:8–13 stresses that both persecution and the proclamation of the gospel are necessary elements in the apocalyptic march of history. Mark's Gospel calls the Roman Christians to follow in the path of the disciples who gave up everything to follow and confess Jesus—and that on the basis of his teaching and the proclamation of his resurrection. They acted on the basis of that alone, not on the proof of resurrection appearances.

The Markan Easter gospel thus both vindicates Jesus' teaching about suffering and confession by pointing to his new position and calls Christians to confess him. Jesus' resurrection is the beginning of the apocalyptic end time. His enthronement has cosmic significance.

But that significance is also a sober warning against an easy apocalyptic that focuses only on the ultimate triumph. Jesus inaugurates the apocalyptic events with his resurrection; the church is called to live out the full apocalyptic program of suffering and confession. 1 Cor. 15:20–28, that vision of the ultimate triumph, is reined in by the serious summons of Mark 16. The Easter gospel in Mark offers a present call to action, not a comfort via future resurrection. Mark balances Paul.

The burden of proclamation on this day is to proclaim the exaltation of the Old Testament and Pauline lessons without muting the immediate significance of the Gospel for our life in the not-yet world, suffering in the throes of apocalyptic oppression. There could also take place the easy transfer of the call from ourselves to others. The temptation would be to preach that people suffering under oppressive, anti-Christian political systems should have the courage to confess their faith. While their confession should encourage American Christians, Mark's message is directed to Americans to confess in the inhibiting context of our own secularist culture. That is no small challenge.

Easter Evening or
Easter Monday

Lutheran	Roman Catholic	Episcopal
Dan. 12:1c–3 or Jon. 2:2–9	Acts 2:14, 22–32	Acts 5:29a, 30–32 or Dan. 12:1–3
1 Cor. 5:6–8		1 Cor. 5:6b–8 or Acts 5:29a, 30–32
Luke 24:13–49	Matt. 28:8–15	Luke 24:13–35

The lectionary does not provide separate lessons for the Easter Vigil service (the true first service of Easter) and Easter morning services. The second set of lessons is scheduled for Easter Day evening or Easter Monday, times rarely observed in most parishes (though seminaries, church-related colleges, and the like may observe them). If the lessons for Easter Day are used for the Vigil, preachers might find the epistle for this day a very helpful text for the service on Easter morning.

FIRST LESSON

Dan. 12:1c–3 is the conclusion to the four great dream visions that make up the second half of the book. (The first six chapters tell six stories about Daniel.) The book is written in a time of severe oppression in Israel, under Antiochus IV Epiphanes, King of the Seleucid empire, with its captial in Antioch. Antiochus, who ruled from 175 to 163 B.C., was an astute ruler who had little understanding of the Jewish people. His great enemy was the Ptolemaic Empire of Egypt. A false rumor of his death in Egypt in 169 B.C. led to a rebellion by the Jews in Jerusalem. In putting the rebellion down Antiochus plundered the temple treasury to fill his own depleted resources. Determined to end the problem of rebellious Jews once and for all, Antiochus embarked on a vigorous program of enforced Hellenization. The story is told in 1 Macc. 1:41–64. Repression called forth both conformity and opposition. Some hurried to adapt; others protested the enforced ban on Yahwism. The protest erupted into guerilla warfare under the Hasmoneans, the sons of Mattathias of Modin. Jewish sacrifices in the temple, which Antiochus had dedicated to Zeus Hypsistos in 167 B.C., were resumed in 164 B.C., after the purification of the temple. The revolt of the Maccabees was successful. (It went on until political independence was secured in 129 B.C. But that story goes far beyond the background to the book of Daniel.)

Daniel is written toward the end of the period in which the temple is defiled (i.e., about 165/64 B.C.). The unknown author writes to encourage the Jewish people in this time of religious oppression. He shares the repugnance of the Maccabees for Antiochus, described as the "little" horn of 7:8, that grew tremendously to the south and the east, even threw down some of the host of the stars, and instituted the "transgression that makes desolate" in the Jerusalem temple (8:11–14), the altar to Zeus. The longest description of him comes in 11:21–45, written with exquisite distaste. He even seeks to seduce "with flattering words those who violate the covenant" (11:32).

Yet Daniel has little that urges people to join in the rebellion led by the Maccabees. He urges the people to endure patiently the suffering that comes on them. Antiochus's end is set for the "time appointed" (11:35). Fidelity is called for. The Jews are not to learn self-reliance, but trust in God, who controls history and the destiny of kings and nations. The four great visions each make that point. The time comes when "one like a son of man" will be enthroned (7:13, 14), when the people of the saints of the Most High will receive the royal rule (7:27). History moves according to the plan of years and weeks ordained by God (9:1–27) until the "decreed end is poured out upon the desolator" (9:27).

The text describes the hope of those who patiently wait for that "decreed end." The great heavenly warrior Michael will arise on behalf of the people. Michael is a great figure in later Jewish apocalyptic (cf. Dan. 10:20, warrior for Israel), whose name is emblazoned on the banner leading one of the four troops of God in the final battle at Qumran (1QM IX. 14–16). He leads the forces of heaven against the Satanic host in Rev. 12:7–9. Michael's appearance means that the end time events have reached their climax. The low point of Israel's history will be reached, but the faithful, that is, those whose names "shall be found written in the book" of life (12:1), shall be delivered. The book is referred to earlier in Dan. 7:10 as open before the Ancient of Days. The motif occurs elsewhere in Ps. 69:28; Exod. 32:32; Rev. 3:5; Phil. 4:3.

But the final outcome would be incomplete unless those who died for their fidelity are included. And God's name would not be glorified if the traitors were not punished. Dan. 12:2 speaks of "many" dead who will be resurrected. The passage sounds a rare note in the Old Testament. A few passages, for example, Isa. 26:19, express hope for the resurrection of the righteous. But Dan. 12:2 is unique in expressing hope for the resurrection of faithful and apostate alike. Those who bore their martyrdom faithfully and patiently will be raised to share the "everlasting life" of God's people. The collaborators of 167–164 B.C. who have died will be raised to "everlasting contempt" (12:2), to exclusion from Israel and the knowledge that they are despised. Their resurrection underscores the fidelity of God (cf. Isa. 66:24) and his justice. The "wise" of 12:3 are the teachers of 11:33 (cf. Isa. 53:11) who encouraged the faithful to endure in suffering. They shall receive a preeminent position. "Stars" is a symbol for heavenly rulers.

The lectionary suggests the omission of 12:1a, the reference to Michael. The omission is inexcusable! Michael is the divine agent for salvation. To omit him is to remove God from the picture. The omission of 12:4 is more defensible, since its literary function is to underscore the esoteric character of the revelation in Daniel. The omission generalizes the knowledge. It occurs out of the conviction expressed in the Gospel for the day, Luke 24:44, 45, that Jesus, the Resurrected, is the hermeneutical key to the understanding of the Old Testament.

SECOND LESSON

The second lesson, 1 Cor. 5:6–8, is a sharp contrast to the first. There is nothing apocalyptic about it. Its language is an application of part of the Passover observance to Christian life. In itself the passage contains no reference to the resurrection of Jesus or to Easter observance in the early Christian church. But it is this passage, used for fifteen or more centuries as the epistle for Easter Sunday, that stimulated the application of paschal language to Easter. Martin Luther's great Easter hymn, *Christ lag in Todesbanden,* provided the text for Bach's Easter cantata (no. 4). Stanzas 3–5 *(LBW,* no. 134) are based on the language of this text. Christians who are not familiar with the context in which it is set must be amazed to discover that it is originally an exhortation against pride based on the conviction of special, superior theological knowledge.

Context is here all-decisive. 1 Cor. 5:1–5 is Paul's demand that the Corinthians deal with a member living "with his father's woman" (5:1); Paul labels the case "fornication." What specially enraged Paul (the verb is not too strong) was that the Corinthians were actually proud (5:2 "you're puffed up"; 5:6: "your boasting is not good") of the man's actions. Their pride is caused by the man taking seriously his baptismal experience. Baptism was regarded as death and resurrection in Christ, a movement from the realm of the body to the realm of the Spirit, from slavery to freedom. (Almost the whole of the Corinthian understanding of Paul's proclamation is based on this premise.) That is why the Corinthians did not expect a resurrection of dead people (15:12), since death is not an evil, but the release of the spirit from the body that is evil. The man lives with his father's wife because his baptismal death freed him from predeath relationships (cf. Rom. 7:1–6); his life with her was done "in the name of the Lord," revising the RSV translation to attach the phrase to "the man who has done such a thing."

Drastic misunderstanding that leads to radically wrong actions demands drastic measures to correct it. 5:3–5 describes a form of church law exercised against the man. 5:6–8 is the justification of the radical action demanded of the congregation. Pride must be removed. "Don't you know that a little leaven leavens the entire lump?" (5:6) is a well-known proverb (cf. Gal. 5:9), equivalent to our saying about the one "rotten apple." The tie to being "puffed up" in 5:2 is visual, dependent on the action of yeast.

The situation demands also some discipline within the church, the community (lump) that is being affected by the "little leaven." Preparations for the Jewish Passover included the removal of all leaven and fermented grain from the house and its storage chambers on the night before the Passover meal is eaten. The *Mishnah, Pesachim* 1.1 states: "On the night of the 14th the *hametz* [any leavened baked goods or any grain that might swell and ferment through contact with liquid] must be searched for by the light of a lamp." There follows a set of regulations as to what is included and how it is to be disposed of. The *Passover Haggadah* (ritual for the celebration) begins with the Passover search for leavened bread and includes a formula to disown any that may accidentally have been missed in the search. The rite illustrates the serious character of Jewish Passover observance of the rule given in Exod. 12:19.

Jesus' death was the death of a Passover lamb (5:7b); therefore the church, the house of God, must be purified of any evil from the old age that might contaminate the festival observance. The death of Jesus shows that there is need for decisive and thorough renovation. There must be a complete removal of all that is old so that the celebration may be pure ("sincerity" literally means that defects are not to be disguised with a coating of wax) and authentic.

Paul applies the language of ritual observance here to life, as he so frequently does (cf. Rom. 12:1–2, 15:16). The measure of Christian worship is not the observance of rituals, but the living out of confession in responsible action. The death of Jesus is the starting point for Christian life, not a theory of the resurrection that removes people from true life in community before God. Put in terms of the Daniel lesson, the work of Michael does not mean the end of fidelity.

It is striking that Paul does not develop any interpretation of this sacrificial language in terms of a theory of salvation or an understanding of the role of Christ. That in itself is enough to warn the preacher off from constructing such theories, even though Luther does so in his Easter hymn. It is not the removal of sin by sacrifice or the deliverance by the blood of the Passover lamb that interests Paul, but the renovation of Christian life that flows from Christ's death. And that is a theme that cannot be overpreached.

GOSPEL

Luke's Easter narrative (24:13–49) is by far the most extensive of any Gospel's. It does not just cover Luke 24, but the whole of the Book of Acts as the continuation of the things that "Jesus began to do and teach" (Acts 1:1). Indeed, Luke 24 is in many ways a preparation for the continuation of the narrative in Acts. That is certainly true of the two narratives that are used as lessons in the Easter cycle, the gospels for Easter Evening and for Ascension, both drawn from Luke 24. That also indicates why the first lesson throughout the Easter cycle is drawn from Acts, the acts not of the disciples, but of the risen Christ and the Spirit.

Luke 24:13–49 is an artistically constructed whole of two major narratives, each of which falls into two scenes. The Emmaus story begins with teaching in the context of a travel narrative (24:13–27) and concludes with a table scene in Emmaus (24:28–35); the Jerusalem story begins with a table scene (24:36–43) and concludes with teaching (24:44–49). The arrangement is not accidental; teaching frames the two meal scenes, a salutary reminder not to regard the meal as predominant in the Emmaus narrative.

These two narratives contain some common themes, important to Lukan theology. The travel narrative (24:13–27) is reminiscent of the great travel narrative in Luke 9:51—19:28. That travel narrative is the setting for the major block of disciple teaching in the Gospel. The teaching of the resurrected Lord also begins on the way. The Book of Acts which follows uses the "way" as a name for the church (Acts 9:2) and speaks of the "way of salvation" (16:17). Luke is enough of a consummate artist that the symbolism might well be intentional.

The way begins in Jerusalem, a city which occupies a special place in Luke's thought. It is the city both where Jesus appears to his disciples and from which the Christian gospel spreads throughout the world. (There is no command to go to Galilee in Luke's resurrection story.) Jerusalem is the place where the disciples are to wait for power, the promise of the father (24:49). It is also the place where the witness to Jesus begins (24:47; Acts 1:4,8; 2:1—8:3). For Luke, Jerusalem is the central city of the church (not Rome, though his narrative tends in that direction).

The Emmaus narrative proposes an answer to the question, How is the resurrected Jesus known? The answer is more complicated than is often thought. First of all, a knowledge of the facts of the case is not enough. Cleopas and his companion (is it perchance his wife?) know the facts well enough. In 24:19–21 they describe Jesus as "from Nazareth, a prophetic man, mighty in word and deed." They put him into the category of Moses ("mighty in word and deed," Acts 7:22) and Elijah (cf. Luke 7:11–17), who raised dead sons to life (1 Kings

17:23; cf. 2 Kings 4:36). They knew the facts of his death at the hands of the religious leaders and the political authorities. His crucifixion dashed their hopes that he was the one to redeem Israel. They reflect the ignorance of the disciples in 9:44–45 and 18:31–34, and do not recall Jesus' repeated affirmation that Jerusalem was the place for a prophet to die (11:49–51; 13:33, 34), or his weeping over the city in 19:41–44. It is clear that they regard their hopes dashed. Yet Jesus had begun his career in Nazareth claiming to be the fulfillment of prophecy and compared himself to both Elijah and Elisha (4:17–21, 25–27). The data are known, their significance is not. The same is true of the Jerusalem disciples (cf. 24:34–38).

Two actions of Jesus enable faith and confession. The first is table fellowship, both in Emmaus (24:28–31) and Jerusalem (24:41–43). Such fellowship is prominent throughout the gospel (cf. 7:34, 36–50; 5:29–32; 15:1–2). The Emmaus meal parallels in particular the feeding of the five thousand in 9:12–17. Both meals take place at late evening, when the day has declined. In both they recline at dinner (the same verb is used); and in both he blesses, breaks, and shares. The messianic banquet of fellowship via prayer (blessing) is here enacted (cf. Mark 14:22). After the feeding Peter confesses Jesus as the Christ; here their eyes are opened.

While it is not common coin to say so, the meal at Emmaus (and the fellowship meals in Acts) are not repetitions of the Passover meal in 22:14–20. There the cup comes first. Before and after that first cup Jesus points out that he will not eat or drink the Passover again until the eschaton. Luke contains no command to repeat the meal. Rather the great era of witness to Jesus is bounded by the first Eucharist of Luke 22 and the expectation of the eschatological Eucharist in the end time. One should make no eucharistic interpretations of the Emmaus scene and talk about the presence of Christ now in the church through the sacrament of holy communion. That may reproduce Pauline theology; Luke knows nothing of it!

The other action that must go with table fellowship is the teaching of Jesus drawn from the Old Testament. That was the burden of the teaching on the road (24:25–27) and also in the upper room after the meal (24:44–47). In the case of the Emmaus disciples, Jesus' actions of praying and sharing made the teaching from the Old Testament significant. In Jerusalem the table fellowship was a response to their lack of faith and is followed by the opening of the Scriptures. The sermons in Acts, especially in the first twelve chapters, are dominated by the argument from the Old Testament. Jesus himself is its initiator according to Luke. Both teaching and experience are needed fully to understand Jesus and confess him.

Such teaching is at the same time Jesus' farewell discourse, like the book of Deuteronomy is for Moses or Genesis 49 is for Jacob. 24:44 is almost a verbal citation of Deut. 1:1. The discourse stresses the significance of the resurrection. It is the basis for the universal proclamation of repentance that leads to salvation in his name (24:47). It also set the disciples on the path of witness that will be traced out in Acts.

Luke 24 is the springboard into the Book of Acts which provides every first lesson in the Sundays of Easter. Acts presents both the teaching that is needed and the witness to the experience of the disciples. Easter proclamation must focus on both of the emphases of Luke. The lesson from 1 Corinthians 5 is a magnificent example of the teaching drawn from the events of Passover and Easter. The Lukan Gospel for the day calls all to believe on the basis of experience of the risen Christ and commitment to his teaching. Neither shallow sentimentalism nor severe moralism measures up to the magnitude of Luke's Gospel. Today it may be in the call to witness that persons will most experience the present power of Christ; the teaching of the pulpit should impel people into that ministry of witness.

The Second Sunday of Easter

Lutheran	Roman Catholic	Episcopal	Pres/UCC/Chr	Meth/COCU
Acts 3:13–15, 17–26	Acts 4:32–35	Acts 3:12a, 13–15, 17–26 or Isa. 26:2–9, 19	Acts 4:32–35	Acts 3:12a, 13–15, 17–26 or Isa. 26:2–9, 19
1 John 5:1–6	1 John 5:1–6	1 John 5:1–6 or Acts 3:12a, 13–15, 17–26	1 John 5:1–6	1 John 5:1–6
John 20:19–31	John 20:19–31	John 20:19–31	Matt. 28:11–20	John 20:19–31

Though it is the year of Mark, the lectionary in Easter takes its lessons almost entirely from Luke and John. The reason is not hard to find. Both Luke and John have accounts of resurrection appearances that illuminate significant aspects of the Christian faith. Both have material that explicitly relates to the life of the post-Easter community: Luke in the narrative of Acts (all of the first lessons for the second through the seventh Sundays of Easter come from Acts 1—11) and John in the "farewell discourses" of Jesus (the lectionary uses chaps. 15 and 17). In Series B the second lessons are all taken from 1 John. One should give serious consideration to preaching a series of sermons either on the Acts sequence or the 1 John sequence, and urging parishioners to read the entire books alongside the sermons. Even better, if Sunday Bible study would concentrate on the work from which the texts are taken, both Bible study and preaching would be enriched by the interaction. In most cases it is not possible to draw any close lines of contact between Acts and the Gospels for these Sundays. The material from 1 John and the Gospels correlates much better—and will be treated in this manner in what follows:

GOSPEL

John 20:19–31 and 1 John 5:1–6 each deal with aspects of the Johannine understanding of faith. The Gospel was written for a church that was afraid, lonesome, feeling abandoned. It had, to use a modern term, an identity crisis. Born inside of Judaism, it discovered that Judaism was now rejecting its child. Christian Jews were being "put out of the synagogue," in some sense formally excommunicated (the term *aposynagogos* occurs three times in John, and only in John: 9:22; 12:42; 16:2). Indeed, "fear of the Jews" was inhibiting discipleship. That fear is reflected in the Gospel in Joseph of Aramathea, who is a secret disciple for "fear of the Jews," 19:38; in Jerusalem, no one spoke openly their good opinion of Jesus "because of fear of the Jews" (7:13). The parents of the blind man healed at the Pool of Siloam were afraid to say what they knew "because they feared the Jews" (9:22). Fear of being put out of the synagogue kept members of the high priestly group from confessing their faith (12:42).

The Gospel of John has a minimum of future eschatology. (Other books written in the same period seem to increase in their use of apocalyptic, e.g., Matthew, Revelation, and 2 Thessalonians.) There seems to be despair of the future in the Johannine community. It expresses itself in loss of hope. And loss of hope leads to a weakening of the Christian confession. John's Gospel faces that situation. Two courses of action were open to the writer. He might have excoriated the community for giving up the faith and its expression inherited from the past and asked them to recover the tradition they had lost. That is not the path he takes. Rather he recognizes the change in situation and writes a Gospel that speaks to a fearful generation.

The Gospel for Easter II is the satisfying and triumphant conclusion of the Gospel. (John 21 is a secondary supplement added to the Gospel by a later writer to deal with the question of the role of Peter.) Recall what has come in the eighteen verses before the text. John's Easter morning narrative circles around the reaction of three people to the resurrection: Peter, the disciple Jesus loved, and Mary Magdalene. John gives the beloved disciple the honor of being the first to believe (20:8). Peter sees the folded grave clothing, but no reaction is ascribed to him. (That may be the reason the later writer added John 21 in an attempt to underscore Peter's role.) Mary of Migdal, the fishing village a few miles southwest of Capernaum on the Sea of Galilee, recognizes Jesus as her *Rabboni,* that is, "teacher" (20:16). But that reaction is inadequate, as Jesus' response to her in the next verse shows. Her confession took no note of his resurrection. For reasons of his own the writer of the Gospel gives no content to the beloved disciple's faith. Thus the narrative of Easter morning requires both correction and supplementation for an adequate understanding of the resurrected Jesus.

Today's Gospel gives that needed addition. Two vignettes of Jesus and his disciples are given to us, followed by a conclusion that sums up the entire Gospel. The first (20:19–23) is the meeting (the first) with the disciples in the locked room on the evening of resurrection day. The scene is full of symbolism and reminiscences of the earlier parts of the Gospel. The disciples have gathered in the closed room out of "fear of the Jews" (20:19). The only other time Jesus is with them in such a gathering is at the banquet in which he gives his farewell discourses (John 13:1—17:26). There Jesus had told them not to be troubled or afraid precisely because he was going away from them (14:1–4, 27–31). Fear and faith do not cohere. Jesus came into their group and said *Shalom,* that is, "Peace be among you" (20:19). The word then, as now, is the common greeting and farewell in the Middle East. But Jesus' greeting is more than mere formality. It recalled his words about peace in the farewell discourses (John 14:27; 16:33); peace is his gift to the disciples.

The problem with the disciples is not that they do not accept the fact of Jesus' resurrection. 20:20 makes clear that the problem is their failure to realize the implications of his resurrection for present existence. He shows them his hands and side (cf. 19:34). "Then the disciples rejoiced because they saw the Lord." The demonstration is not to establish table fellowship as in Luke 24. John makes clear already in his conclusion to the crucifixion that the wounds of Jesus awaken faith. John 19:35: "What he has seen, he has testified, and his testimony is true, and he knows that he speaks true things, in order that you may believe." They know his resurrection and still are afraid. But the sight of his wounds brings joy, the new thing, the antithesis of fear.

The loss of fear leads to a second great gift on Jesus' part. He introduces it with another *shalom* (v. 21). Jesus had prayed in his great prayer: "Sanctify them by truth; your *logos* is truth. Just as you sent me into the world, I also sent them into the world" (John 17:17–18). Jesus now actualizes that prayer (20:21) by a significant action. He "breathed into" them *(enephysēsen)* and said, "Take holy spirit" (John 20:22). Great traditions lie behind this action. The verb "breathe into" is the verb used of the life-giving action of God into Adam (Gen. 2:7; Wis. of Sol. 15:11 says he breathed in a "lively spirit"). Ezek. 37:9 uses the verb of sending the spirit into the valley of dry bones. To breathe in means to set the creative power of God into action. John had spoken of this spirit earlier. While Jesus was with the disciples in his ministry, "the Spirit was not yet, because Jesus was not yet glorified" (7:39). He said this about the Spirit those who believe in him were going to get. John describes Jesus' death in the phrase "he handed over the Spirit" (19:30). That is, Jesus' death is his glorification (cf. John 3:14; 17:1–5). Therefore his death also means the fulfillment of the word in 7:39. At the cross were his mother and the disciple he loved (19:25–27), along with other women. They are not far off as in the Synoptic tradition. In their new relation (son/mother) they are the community that receives the Spirit handed over at Jesus' glorification. Now the disciples (who were not close to the cross) receive the Spirit as the believing community (7:39).

20:23 makes clear John's understanding of the Spirit. He does not do pyrotechnical things in John, like the performance of miracles or speaking tongues. John knows of no such deeds by the disciple community. Rather the Spirit carries forward through the community the message and the work of Jesus. They are to forgive and retain sins. In John *the* sin is unbelief (John 3:17–18; 16:8–11). Jesus as the Lamb of God takes away the sin of the world (1:29, 36).

Easter is tied closely to the cross in John. They together are the great act of salvation. But Easter for John is more than resurrection. In this one act of being lifted on the cross and raised from the dead there is also the Johannine ascension and the Johannine Pentecost.

Easter is the exaltation of Jesus and the giving of the Spirit. Thus the Johannine Gospel impels the proclamation of the close tie between Jesus and the Spirit, between the disciple community and the present power of the Resurrected One. It is this understanding of Easter that removes fear, comforts the community that feels abandoned, assures the community that it is not left alone. It has the Paraclete, the great companion of the church, as its power and co-worker. The church is not abandoned, but accompanied.

The second scene (John 20:24–29) marks an advance on the first. It is the familiar story of Thomas. Earlier in the Gospel he is presented as one who fails to understand what Jesus is about (11:16; 14:5). He refuses to accept the testimony of the disciples (they are about the business of removing unbelief). Thomas is the unbeliever in this conclusion. He asks for proof of the witness (20:24–25). In a scene much like the first, Jesus comes and gives it to him (20:26–27). He introduces his words once again with *shalom,* the word that prefaces a revelation. He invites Thomas to get the proof he asked for, "and be not faithless, but believing" (20:27). Thomas responds with the capstone confession of the Gospel, "My Lord and my God" (20:28). Again the tradition behind this confession is striking. The two titles occur in the Shema, the Jewish credo drawn from Deut. 6:4: "Hear, O Israel: The Lord our God is one Lord." Thus the Old Testament is drawn upon. But at this same time the Roman emperor Domitian, according to the Roman historian Suetonius (*Dom.* XIII.2), was addressed as "Our Lord and our God." For Christians Jesus now has this role. This is the first time this confession is made in the Gospel, though John 1:1 had spoken it out in the prologue. Chap. 1 of the Gospel has many titles applied to Jesus; there is no messianic secret. But his ultimate title is the one Thomas gives. Thomas has moved from unbelief to faith.

The last three verses of the Gospel spell out the significance of all this. Thomas required proof. For him seeing was believing. Jesus pronounces a *makarism* on those who believe on the basis of witness alone. The preeminent witness is the Gospel of John itself, as 20:30–31 makes clear. There could have been a much longer gospel, if quantity were what counted. But John has given what one needs to know to believe and have eternal life in Christ's name.

The preaching values of this magnificent text lie in its insistence that Easter releases the Spirit into the church. That Spirit does not produce or require great deeds, but faith. Faith is life in the certainty of the presence of Christ in our world. The church is here, in the middle of people who feel fear, lonesomeness, futility, and estrangement from God, themselves, one another, and life. John reminds us that it is not adequate to preach only a future hope. His message is that there is change, life, and joy in the present. Christians are the means by which the Spirit is active in the present. Jesus risen and ascended does not mean an orphaned church. God who was in the flesh is the giver of Spirit to all who believe. Glory has become present in our world— through us!

SECOND LESSON

1 John 5:1–5 interprets and expands the message of the Gospel. That is even true in terms of its origins. The letter was written in the declining days of the first century to prevent a false interpretation of John's Christ. One way of dealing with the hostile world is to deny that it has any significant relevance. That was done in the first century by people who drew a sharp line between the Spirit and the flesh/body, between existence in the realm of revealed power and existence in the realm of our physical world. Whether this was already a gnostic system in the later first century can be debated. Certainly in the second century Gnostics were using the Gospel of John to defend this opinion. 1 John writes to prevent the use of a false Christology in support of this heresy. It does it in the lesson for today by making two major points. (1) Faith and love must be kept together. Any tendency to define faith only in terms of knowledge of God or of union with God that deserts the practical, earthy implications of faith is wrong. (2) Any belief in Christ that is used to justify such an attitude is wrong.

1 John 5:1–4 stresses the relationship of faith and love. "Every one who believes that Jesus is the Christ has been born of God" (1:1). Belief means more for this letter than acceptance of something as true, a kind of passive intellectual affirmation. Faith is an active relationship to God that also establishes other contact points. The verb "believe" is frequent in the last three chapters of 1 John (3:23; 4:1, 16; 5:1, 5, 10, 13). Faith is directed toward the Son of God, the Christ. Thus any faith is misshapen that is not formed by who the Son of God is. The text stresses that Jesus is the Christ, that is, that the very human, fleshly Jesus is the Christ. That is the confession that we make, that "Jesus is the Son of God" (4:15). Jesus cannot be reduced to an idea or a disembodied spirit, to a heavenly emanation from God, as the Gnostics do. Nothing less than our childhood from God is at stake. To be a child of God is to be involved in this world, to "do righteousness" (2:29). To be a child of God is to be like Jesus (3:2–3).

To be a child is to love the father (5:1b). Faith is the presupposition of love, because faith sees our tie to Jesus who is the Son par excellence. That love will also extend to the other children of the family. V. 2 restates that position by making the love of God ("whenever we love God") the touchstone ("By this . . . ") to measure or evaluate whether we in fact love the children of God. At first glance this seems to stand the argument on its head. Ought not the love for God's children be the standard by which we measure the love of God? The last clause makes the underlying rationale clear. Love for God is not a formless, vague, warm feeling; nor is it an intellectual approval of God's being; nor is it a mystical involvement or absorption into God. Rather love for God is equated with "we . . . obey his commandments" (5:2) The motif occurs earlier in 1 John (2:3–4; 3:14; cf. 2 John 6; John 14:15, 21). It always has the same content: love of fellow Christians.(1 John 3:22, 23 uses the term of believing in him and loving one another.) It is striking that 1 John nowhere uses any of the ethical lists or maxims of Hellenistic ethics, as Paul, 1 Peter, and other writers do. For this writer, ethics is reduced to this one command.

Vv. 3–4 stress that this command is not difficult (v. 3) because of the presupposition of faith. Faith is not vague and formless, but directed to Christ and his work. Therefore it begins with the conviction that the cosmos, the world that is hostile to God and divorced from him, has been defeated. Faith in Christ is not some naive optimism about humankind or some idealistic view of ethical possibilities. Faith conquers because Christ conquers. Faith is equivalent to our confession, 3:14.

That confession is clarified in 5:5–6. The one who conquers is the one who believes that Jesus is the Son of God, the Christ (cf. 5:1; 4:15; 2:22). The antignostic character of that confession is made clear in 5:6. Jesus, the Son of God, came by both water and blood. Some tie to the historical, physical, earthly Jesus is meant. Some interpreters point to John 19:34 and argue that this means 1 John refers to his death on the cross. But the division between water and blood in the second half of the statement argues against that interpretation. It is more likely a rejection of the idea that Jesus, the man, is to be distinguished from Christ, God's son, who is heavenly and pneumatic. At Jesus' baptism the descending Spirit is the descent of the heavenly on the man. On the cross the Spirit leaves to return to God, while the man Jesus dies. In the gnosticizing Gospel of Peter Jesus on the cross shouts, "My power, my power, you have deserted me!" just before he dies. That power is the ascendant spirit. Thus blood refers to death. Both bap-

tism and the cross are means by which the Son of God came in the
form of the fleshly Jesus. The Spirit supports that by his testimony,
which is truth. That testimony must be the confession of Jesus as the
Son of God, which people make by the Spirit (cf. 4:2).

The Johannine letter reinforces the Gospel by connecting faith and
living (love). It justifies that tie by referring to the character of Jesus
himself. The powerful Resurrected One is the earthly one. Therefore,
his significance must also be earthly, down in our world.

FIRST LESSON

Acts 3:13–15, 17–26 is part of a sequence in Acts that provides the
first lesson for three Sundays in Easter. It therefore deserves some
careful attention. (Careful readers cannot help but notice that the
treatments of the lessons for Easter II have been longer than those for
Easter Day and Easter Monday. That is because these three books,
Acts, 1 John, and John, provide the majority of lessons in Easter for
Series B.)

The text forms the second of Peter's great sermons in Acts. (The
first is the Pentecost sermon in 2:14–36.) The precipitating incident is
the cure of the lame man at the Beautiful Gate of the temple (3:1–10).
The story makes clear that Peter and John had no power themselves;
rather the name of Jesus Christ, invoked by Peter, effects the cure
(3:6). The man's reaction is to run and leap in praise of God. The
people in the temple precinct run together to the Stoa of Solomon.
This was the great portico, two stories high, with three aisles, on the
south side of the temple precinct. It ranks as one of the great stoas of
the ancient world.

Peter seizes the opportunity to address the people who have run
together. (The text for the lesson omits v. 12, the introduction to the
sermon, and v. 16; the omission of the latter is indefensible. It refers to
the name of Jesus and the faith of the lame man.) The sermon falls into
two main sections, 3:12–16 and 3:17–26. The two sections are quite
different in spirit.

The first part of the sermon is christologically oriented. It reflects
Luke's singular view of Jesus' death and resurrection in relation to the
church and the Jewish people. In that sense it is Luke's model for
proclamation to non-Christian Jews. (It should be stressed that this
does not provide *the* mode for Christian-Jewish contact and dialogue
today.) Peter makes clear that he is addressing the Jewish people with
his opening: ''Men of Israel'' (3:12). He rejects any suggestion that
John and he had any personal power or piety that could have cured the

lame man (3:12). Rather God must receive credit for what he has made present in the world through Jesus. The scene is the temple, the place where the Lord caused his name to dwell (Deut. 12:11). It is the earlier location for Jesus' teaching in Jerusalem (Luke 20:1—21:37, especially 37; the little apocalypse in Mark 13 is spoken on the Mount of Olives, and only to the inner circle of disciples). After the ascension the disciples worshiped and praised God in the temple (Luke 24:53; Acts 2:46). Now it becomes the place where Jesus is proclaimed by them.

God, who is worshiped in the temple, is named in the ancient formula of Exod. 3:6 (v. 13). He has glorified "his servant Jesus." The sermon accounts for Jesus in terms of the suffering and exalted Righteous One of the Old Testament (cf. Wisdom of Solomon 2—5; Daniel 7), especially the "Servant of the Lord" in Isa. 52:13—53:12. The Septuagint of Isa. 52:13 uses the verb "glorify" of God's action. That is now applied to Jesus, who is also called "the Holy and Righteous One" (3:14; cf. 7:52, 22:14) and the "Pioneer of life" (3:15). The scheme of thought is clear. Jesus died because the Jews denied him ("deny" is the antonym to "confess") and turned him over to Pilate. Pilate wanted to release him (3:13; cf. Luke 23:4, 14–15, 22, where Pilate pronounces Jesus innocent, and 23:24, where the death sentence is simply catering to the crowd's demands). Jesus first, like the missionaries later, is innocent in the eyes of Roman judges. Jesus' death is an evil, a miscarriage of justice for which Jews are responsible (cf. Acts 2:23, 36; 4:10; 5:30; 10:39; 13:27–28). But God reversed their evil act by raising Jesus from the dead. Thus he glorified Jesus (3:13) and gave him the position of "Lord and Messiah" (Acts 2:36). Thus we meet a peculiar Lukan stress, quite different from Paul and John. John regards Jesus' death as stage 1 in his glorification (see the exposition of the Gospel for Easter II). Paul frequently uses formulas that regard Jesus' death as a sin-removing sacrifice (Rom. 3:24–26; 4:25; 1 Cor. 15:3–5). But Luke does not regard the death of Jesus as atoning. His account of the Lord's Supper does not include the words which interpret the cup as the "blood shed for the remission of sins" (Luke 22: 17–19; the RSV correctly omits v. 20 as a later harmonizing interpolation). In Lukan thought the great act of God is the resurrection which sets right the evil of Jesus' crucifixion. The Risen Lord made his disciples "witnesses" (3:15) to that. It is the power of the exalted Resurrected One whose name is able to cure the lame man. The man simply believed (3:16). There is a slight problem here, since 3:1–10 says nothing of faith on the lame man's part. Luke by the term "faith" underscores the gracious character of the act. There is no human responsibility for it.

Witnesses is what the disciples are (1:22; 2:32; 4:33; 10:41; 13:31; 22:15), but that witness also involves what Peter does in the second part of the sermon (3:17–26). He turns to appeal to the Jews. Their evil act was done out of ignorance (3:17), but God, who announced the necessity of the suffering of the Anointed One in advance by the prophets, carried out the plan to the end. "Suffer" here means to die, as it does in 1:3; Luke 24:26, 46; and 1 Pet. 3:18. The status of the resurrected Jesus means that repentance and forgiveness are available (Acts 3:19), as Jesus had said in Luke 24:47. It is there for all nations, beginning with Jerusalem. Jesus' resurrection means that he is in heaven. Until he returns (1:11) there is forgiveness for those who repent. When he returns he will carry out the task of Elijah, the restitution of all things (v. 21; Mal. 3:1; 4:5–6). But now the words of Moses about the prophet like himself (3:22–23; Deut. 18:15–18; Lev. 23:29) apply. Listen to him. Vv. 25–26 suggest that the Jews, as children of the prophets and the covenant with Abraham (note the reference to Gen. 12:3), still have priority in the plan of God (this against a suggestion of anti-Semitism in Luke). The resurrection of Jesus shows that the Servant of the Lord brings blessings to all Israelites who repent. Their repentance will even hasten the coming of the days of refreshment referred to in 3:19–21.

All of this has some eminently preachable insights, useful in the present. Luke reminds us that an absent Christ is not a weak Christ. It is only in his name that witnesses have any power. But the converse is also true. The acts of benefaction done in the name of Jesus are deeds of Christ. The Christian community is thus the dispenser of God's power in the world. This does not ennoble the church as though it has a possession to manage; rather it puts the church under the obligation to witness to the Resurrected One. The form of that witness will vary in every age, but the witness is not optional. Luke's narrative also shows that the witness must include the physical well-being of people and the world. Salvation includes the body.

Second, in an age where eschatology seems to be difficult to proclaim, both Luke and John stress that the present age has eschatological significance in the actions of the church, that is, of the witnesses to Christ. In John the church is the place where the forgiving Spirit is at work. In Luke the understanding of Jesus as the returning Elijah, the expectation of the coming "restoration of all things," is prefigured in the holistic ministry of the church. Luke makes clear that the power for that ministry does not lie in the degree of moral indignation or the feelings of pity that evil or need arouse. Rather Luke makes clear that the ministry must be that of the resurrected Christ, who alone is the power for change. That change is so effective in that power that it can not only overturn the crucifixion, but call the crucifiers to repentance and forgiveness. The church often feels uncomfortable with the category of "ignorance" introduced by Luke. We find it difficult to use that category in our understanding of the "enemies" of democracy and the American way. It is striking that the first sermons in Acts were directed to those accused of being the most direct enemies of Jesus. The renovating power of witness will not allow our natural enmities to predominate. The restoration of all things puts our enemies directly within the circle of our concern.

The Third Sunday of Easter

Lutheran	Roman Catholic	Episcopal	Pres/UCC/Chr	Meth/COCU
Acts 4:8–12	Acts 3:13–15, 17–19	Acts 4:5–12 or Mic. 4:1–5	Acts 3:13–15, 17–19	Acts 4:5–12 or Mic. 4:1–5
1 John 1:1—2:2	1 John 2:1–5a	1 John 1:1—2:2 or Acts 4:5–12	1 John 2:1–6	1 John 1:1—2:6
Luke 24:36–49	Luke 24:35–48	Luke 24:36b–48	Luke 24:36–49	Luke 24:35–49

FIRST LESSON

The first lesson, Acts 4:5–12, arises directly out of last week's first lesson, though the lectionary does not make that explicit. The text is Peter's speech to the Jewish council at a hearing, called to investigate his healing of the lame man and his preaching (3:1–26). The stage is set in the first seven verses of chap. 4. Peter and John (and perhaps also the healed lame beggar, as v. 14) are placed under arrest by the priests (responsible for activity in the temple), the officer in charge of the temple police (cf. Acts 5:24, 26), and the Sadducees. The major opponents of Christianity according to Luke are all present (Luke places the Pharisees in this case on the side of the Christians; cf. 5:17,

34). Luke says that the arrest arose from the disciples' teaching of the people and their proclamation of Jesus' resurrection of the dead. They are put in the holdover for the night in expectation of the trial the next day. Luke adds at this point a note about the success of their preaching to the people (4:4): five thousand who heard the word (the missionary proclamation) believed. The figure is probably intended to be added to the three thousand mentioned in 2:41. In any case the number is phenomenally large for a city that probably had a maximum population of some forty thousand people. The point, of course, is that bold proclamation of repentance and forgiveness in the name of Jesus is effectual.

The next morning the High Council of Seventy-one assembles (4:5–6) and the disciples and the healed beggar are set before them. The grounds for the arrest in v. 2 are not mentioned. Instead they inquire of them, "By what power or by what name did you do this, men of your sort?" (The position of the emphatic *hymeis* in the Greek question is sarcastic!)

Peter's reply (our text) is apologetic, not missionary. The "name" is still significant, as in chap. 3, but another term also becomes important here: *boldness* (4:13). The question put is scarcely a strong judicial question; no accusation is implied (though some commentators have supposed that they were being quietly accused of using demonic powers, black magic; cf. Luke 11:15). Peter is filled with the Holy Spirit. The promise of Luke 12:11–12 is fulfilled: "And when they bring you before the synagogues and the rulers and authorities, do not be anxious how or what you are to answer or what you are to say; for the Holy Spirit will teach you in that very hour what you ought to say." Thus Peter is given a special gift for the moment.

His answer falls into two parts, joined by a christological affirmation. He addresses the council respectfully. He suggests that it is a bit absurd if the name or power by which the sick man has been cured (the Greek term is *sesōstai*)—a good act—is really what the trial is about (4:9). The absurdity is only hinted at, but not stated. Peter uses the question to make a pointed statement about Jesus in 4:10. It is the name of Jesus the Anointed from Nazareth, through whom the man has been set before the council healthy. Jesus is named both as the Anointed, that is, the hoped-for Messiah, and as "the Nazarene," a term that reminds one of the angel's message in Mark 16:6. Jesus is further identified by a pair of antithetical relative clauses that have the ring of creedal statements. Jesus is the one "whom you crucified, whom God raised from the dead.'' Thus Luke repeats the schema of death as an evil inflicted on Jesus by the Jews and set right by God's act of raising him from the dead (cf. 2:23–24, 32, 36; 3:13–15). God's vindication has established Jesus as the savior. That should be made known to the entire people Israel. It is the power and the name of the resurrected Jesus that saved the man.

The council's question is thereby answered. But Peter goes on to present a witness to Jesus drawn from Scripture. Peter's interpretation of Jesus' death and resurrection argues that Jesus is alive, not dead; approved by God, not rejected. In one sense Jesus' role as savior is demonstrated by the healthy beggar standing before the council. That demonstration is supported by Peter's reference to Ps. 118:22. ''The stone which the builders rejected is become the head of the corner.'' Jesus is the stone because the religious leaders Peter is addressing have rejected him. Therefore he has been exalted by God to the keystone in the structure. The passage originally referred either to defeated Jerusalem or the defeated nation that would be vindicated by God. Qumran identified itself as ''the precious corner stone, whose foundations shall neither rock nor sway in their place'' (1QS. VIII. 7–8). Christians early applied the stone to Jesus (cf. Luke 20:17; Mark 12:10; 1 Pet. 2:4, 7). As the ''Servant of the Lord'' title originally belonged to the nation, but was transferred to Christ, so too the stone metaphor was also transferred. Peter now draws the conclusion, 4:12: ''So there is salvation [whether health or religious salvation] in no other one. For there is no other name under heaven that has been given among human beings by which it is necessary that we be saved.'' Thus the answer to the question has been expanded to include a universal claim for Christ. If salvation in the sense of health is present in his name—and the beggar is the evidence it is—then salvation in a religious sense must also be in the power and authority of that name.

The rest of the narrative can be summarized rapidly. The councilors are amazed that ''uneducated, common men'' could speak with such *parrhesia* (4:13). The term denotes freedom of speech, boldness, unfettered openness. They identified them as followers of Jesus from their speaking style. (This seems to contradict the first reason given for their arrest, 4:2.) Since they could not deny the fact of the man's cure (4:14), they deliberated in closed session about the best course of action. To prevent the further spread of such influences among the people they determined to threaten Peter and John and so intimidate them (4:15–17). When confronted with the threat (v. 18), Peter and John responded that they bore the responsibility for the threat in the face of God's requirement that they must speak (4:19–20). Threats are repeated, but the council cannot do any more because the people glorified God for the miracle.

The function of this narrative in Acts is to underscore the necessity, the right and duty, the disciples have to proclaim the name. No leader, whether religious or secular, has the authority to compel silence. The power of the resurrected Jesus is such that it comes to confession even in the face of oppression. The missionary proclamation of the risen Christ has a powerful effect, both to save and cure and to awaken fear and repression. There are many voices today that call for the restriction of the message of God to "spiritual matters" and that try to contain the proclamation within the channels and walls of small-minded people. Proclamation of this text demands the careful analysis of such counter authorities in our society, the demonstration that they have rejected God's Anointed One, and the proclamation of Jesus and his power as the bringer of newness and healing to people who are crippled and sick. The opposing forces are present. It is the task of preachers to identify them in the form they take in parish and in society, and to call the Risen Christ to people to stir them up to witness.

GOSPEL

The Gospel for this Sunday, Luke 24:36–49, correlates well with the lesson from Acts. It is a curious feature of Series B that this Gospel is used three times: 24:13–49 is the Gospel for Easter Monday, 24:44–53 for the Ascension, and 24:36–49 for Easter II. The longer texts have been discussed in the relevant sections under those two days. No extensive discussion will be provided here.

However, some comments should be made about the way in which the Gospel correlates with the lesson from Acts. The risen Christ's last act with his disciples before the ascension is his opening of their minds to understand the Scriptures. The Scriptures show that it is God's plan that his Christ should die and be raised, and that repentance unto forgiveness of sins be proclaimed in his name to all the nations beginning from Jerusalem. This commission correlates with what Peter proclaimed in his temple sermon. But in speaking to the council Peter does not proclaim repentance and forgiveness, though the death and resurrection of Jesus, the name, and the universal significance of Jesus are all stressed.

The text in Acts, when correlated with Luke 24, thus raises questions that were not immediately apparent from reading Acts 4 in isolation. The reaction of the Jewish population of Jerusalem and Peter's statement, " Let it be known to you all and to all the people . . ." (4:10), underscore the tie of the Gospel to Judaism. The church dare not overlook the people of the Covenant. "How odd of God/To choose the Jews!" is Ogden Nash's bit of doggerel. Someone, unknown to me by name, capped that distich with the quatrain

> How odd of men
> That when they choose
> They take the God,
> But not the Jews.

Acts 4 and Luke 24 together offer an opportunity to speak a word about the tie of the church to Judaism.

Luke 24 raises a more difficult question than Acts. Is the omission of all reference to repentance and forgiveness in the text Luke's model for apologetic? There is, strictly speaking, no proclamation of good news to the Great Council in Acts 4, only condemnation. Responsible preaching will note that, only to ask whether the proclamation then was adequate, even in an apologetic discourse. Within the literary intention of Luke in chap. 4, the speech is fine and defensible. But it dare not become a model for relationships with non-Christian opponents of the church.

SECOND LESSON

While the Gospel and first lesson are directed to the question of the church's proclamation of Christ, the second lesson (1 John 1:1—2:2) looks into the church's life to examine it in the brilliant light of God's own nature. It is an extremely rich text. It falls into two sections. 1:1–4 is the prologue to the entire book, in which the writer sets out his own credentials for what he is doing, the essential content of his tract, and his purpose. Each of these deserves some comment.

The writer bases his testimony on the fact that he has been involved with the message (note the neuter in 1:1, 3) "from the beginning" (1:1) in a direct, close manner (heard, seen, beheld, handled). The reminiscences of John 1:1 are clear, as is the reminder of John 1:14 ("we beheld his glory") in the use of the unusual verb "behold." The message is tied to a very real, substantive history. The writer's credentials rest on personal involvement in that history, not on an idea.

This involvement authorizes his message ("What we have seen and heard we announce to you," 1:3). It also determines the content of the message: the "word of life" (1:1) as interpreted in 1:2. This word is the writer's proclamation and interpretation of what he has seen. It is based upon the "manifestation" of life that was "with the Father" (cf. John 1:18: "who is in the bosom of the Father"). The life is eternal, that is, salvific. The entire tract we call 1 John is the witness to that eternal life. Therefore the paragraph is the introduction to the whole. The aim of his message is that his readers have fellowship (mutual participation) with him. That involves also fellowship with the Father and with his Son. The word "Son" is the first direct indication in the book that what the writer announces has a personal face (1:3). The idea of fellowship is important to both 1 John and the Gospel of John, though the Gospel never uses the term. Fellowship is accomplished when the message 1 John urges remains in the readers, and they in it. "And so you remain in the Son and in the Father" (2:24). The Gospel speaks of this fellowship under the picture of vine and branches (John 15:1–16; see Gospel for Easter V and VI), or of "remaining" in the Son and the Father (17:21–23). If fellowship is present, then joy also will be there (1 John 1:4).

Proclamation will pick up on this motif of authenticity. It is not the literary ability of the preacher or his or her winsome character that gives authenticity to the Christian message. It is only witness to the event personalized in Christ that gives credibility to proclamation. That is important for both proclaimer and hearer. It is the task of proclamation to make the witness clear, pointed to the situation of the hearer. It is the goal of the hearer to grasp the witness in its fullness and wonder. Great preaching requires committed witness that arises out of personal experience of the manifested life. It also requires great hearers, equally committed to the fellowship with the One proclaimed.

The second half of the lesson (1:5—2:2) focuses on the maintenance of that fellowship with God in the face of sin. The writer is a realist, who knows that Christians live in the actual tainted cosmos. How do they deal with sin? He begins by giving a fundamental message (1:5), that God is light, that no darkness of any kind is in him. The phrase is not a "definition" of God. Rather, it describes God in relation to women and men. Light is used in the Old Testament to describe God's holiness and transcendent being. Creation began with the making of light (Gen. 1:3). God clothes himself in light (Ps. 104:2) as a symbol of his majesty. His light reveals: "In thy light we see light" (Ps. 36:9). Light can be a symbol for salvation (Ps. 27:1), and so the Servant of the Lord is to be a "light for the nations" (Isa. 49:6), so that his salvation may go to the end of the earth. The *logos* is the "light of human beings" (John 1:4), the "authentic light that illuminates every person" (John 1:9); that light came into the darkness of the universe. To follow him means to "walk in light" (John 8:12). The language shifts into the language of ethical action. To do the wrong is to love the darkness more than the light, because one's deeds are evil (John 3:19). He who does the truth comes to the light (John 3:21). John 12:35–36, 46 makes the ethical implications of Jesus' message clear in terms of light. (There is a similar use of light and darkness at Qumran, which sets up a light/dark dualism to account for the split in Judaism; see 1QS. III. 13–IV.1 and the use of the language throughout 1QM.)

1 John 1:6–10 shows the terrible effects on fellowship if Christians erect little parasols of evasion against the light. The three parasols are (1) claiming fellowship with God, but walking in the darkness, that is, not letting our confession affect our life (1:6; cf. John 3:20, 21; "walk" in the sense of living occurs again in 1:7; 2:6, 11). The first parasol is a dichotomy between word and action. (2) The second parasol is to claim that baptism and the Spirit have removed us from the realm of sin and so we do not sin. (John does not specifically credit this to baptism and the gift of the Spirit.) Christians may plead a false sense of arrival at the goal (1:8). (3) The third parasol is to deny that sin has ever had or been a force in one's life (1:10), that is, to contradict both human experience and divine revelation. The effect of such parasol raising is to make liars of ourselves and not to do the truth (the word requires correlative action, 1:6), is to practice self-deception and not have the truth in us (i.e., the message has no real force, 1:8), is to make God a liar and then his word of life is not in us as a force (1:10).

John's view is both realistic and demanding. He recognizes that sin is present and must be dealt with. He also knows that the goal is a life that does not sin (2:1). Our delusions about sin are not adequate to deal with it. Only the sacrifice of Jesus is adequate to remove sin. Fellowship with God grows out of the purification effected by Jesus' blood (1:7; cf. Rom. 3:24–26). Confession of sin discovers that God is faithful to his promise and righteous; he removes our sin in agreement with Jesus' sacrifice (1:9). Finally, we are not left alone in our attempts to deal with our sin. Jesus is our Paraclete, the one who is called as our aid in speaking to God. (All occurrences of the term *"paraclete"* other than this refer to the "other paraclete," the Spirit whom Christ will send: John 14:16, 26, 15:26; 16:7.) The Paraclete Jesus is the "righteous one," that is, the one whose crucifixion and subsequent resurrection remove sin (the title is used in early Christianity of Jesus in Acts 3:14; 7:52; 22:14). His death is the sacrifice that covers sin par excellence. It is there for the entire world. The preaching value of this paragraph should be very clear. It prevents a triumphalist understanding of Christian life. Christians are not distinguished by their superior life style (desirable as that might be), but by their dependence on forgiveness. While the language of sacrifice as a cultic act for the removal of guilt and sin is far removed from our life and experience—possibly even from our reality index— the reality of the gap between our expectancies of life, and what we experience and do, makes this text immediately relevant.

It also underscores the fact that the grand language, almost incoherent, of the prologue is not left in the far reaches of eloquent rhetoric, but is practical and reaches down into prosaic, workaday life. The maintenance of our relation to God and one another is not dependent on our abilities and effort, but upon the forgiving sacrifice of Jesus. That impels us into fellowship with God, his Son, and one another. That fellowship carries out the commandment of love.

The Fourth Sunday of Easter

Lutheran	Roman Catholic	Episcopal	Pres/UCC/Chr	Meth/COCU
Acts 4:23–33	Acts 4:8–12	Acts 4:(23–31) 32–37 or Ezek. 34:1–10	Acts. 4:8–12	Acts 4:23–37 or Ezek. 34:1–10
1 John 3:1–2	1 John 3:1–2	1 John 3:1–8 or Acts 4:(23–31) 32–37	1 John 3:1–3	1 John 3:1–8
John 10:11–18	John 10:11–18	John 10:11–16	John 10:11–18	John 10:11–18

GOSPEL

Easter IV is the annual remembrance of Christ as the Good Shepherd. The popularity of the picture is in some sense surprising, since most Americans no longer have any real contact with pastoral life. The danger is to sentimentalize the picture and so to trivialize it. The Gospel, John 10:11–18, protects against that by picking up and developing Old Testament themes. It is in some ways a pity that none of the great Old Testament texts were selected for the first lesson. It becomes part of the proclamatory task to weave the Old Testament hope into the interpretation of the Johannine text.

God is the shepherd of the people, his flock (Ps. 23:1; 95:7; 74:1; 78:52). He is the shepherd of Israel, who leads Joseph like a flock (Ps. 80:1). Isa. 40:10–11 combines the ideas of God as the warrior-ruler and the shepherd who "will feed his flock like a shepherd, . . . will gather the lambs in his arms." The leaders of Israel are also Israel's shepherds: Moses (Isa. 63:11), David (Ps. 78:70–72), and the one whom Moses is to appoint, "who will go out before them and come in before them, who shall lead them out and bring them in; that the congregation of the Lord may not be as sheep which have no shepherd" (Num. 27:17). It is not surprising that the future hope of Israel is portrayed as the hope for shepherds after God's own heart (Jer. 3:15; 23:1–4!) and that the Messiah is pictured as a shepherd (Ezek. 34:23; 37:24). About 50 B.C. a pious Jew described the messianic king as one who "shepherds the flock of Yahweh in fidelity and righteousness and will not allow one to grow weak among them in their pasture" (Ps. Sol. 17:45).

John 10:11–18 picks up some of this Old Testament language. Jesus is the good shepherd (10:11, 14) in contrast to the hired shepherd, who leaves the flock to the wolves. Jesus protects the sheep. Thus the motif of Jer. 23:1–4 is picked up, as is the protection theme illustrated in Ps. Sol. 17:45. But some things from the Old Testament picture are absent. There is no king language related to shepherd. Instead the shepherd is one who "risks his life" (for this translation cf. Judg. 12:3; 1 Sam. 19:5) for the sheep in the face of danger (John 10:11–13). The character of the shepherd is shown in his priorities: the sheep come before his own life. Thus the stress in the first explication of the good shepherd lies not on the tenderness or affection the shepherd shows, but in his risk on their behalf. (John 10:11–14 does not yet clarify that this shepherd has *actually* laid down his life.)

The repetition of the phrase "I am the good shepherd" in 10:11 indicates a new stage in the good shepherd speech. No longer is the flock the nation, as in the Old Testament, or even the faithful among the people. "I know my own and my own know me" (10:14) is a phrase that marks off Jesus' sheep. They are ones in a special relation to him, as he is in a special relationship to his Father (10:15). Knowledge is not information here, but the special relationship that exists between two. The sheep are the shepherd's own, his possession, because they know him as he knows them (10:14). There is a mutual appreciation based on unity of the Son and the Father expressed in the risk of the shepherd's life for the sheep. The value of the sheep to the shepherd results in a new evaluation of the shepherd by the sheep. Such a relationship transcends national or racial boundaries, as 10:16 makes clear. The good shepherd is defined by his relation to the sheep; the flock is defined by the relationship to the shepherd. Therefore, sheep from another sheepfold nevertheless join the one flock, because they are defined too by the one shepherd. John's Gospel is clearly written within the context of the gentile mission; it argues as firmly as does Ephesians 2 for the given unity of the church on the basis of the one shepherd (cf. 11:52; 17:20).

10:17–18 expands on the theme "to risk his life." Now it is made clear that it means to die. But death is determined by the relationship to the Father. The Father's love determines the shepherd's action. Thus it is not the character of the sheep that motivates the shepherd. His death is an expression of his relation to God. But it is not final! "I have authority to take it again." Thus his death, to use the latei language of the Gospel, is part of his glorification precisely because he is doing the will of the Father. His death is not caused by the powers of fate or destiny (concepts prevalent in this world); his death and life again are the mark of his freedom that reveals the will (charge) of the Father (10:18).

The shepherd language here is thus anything but sentimental. Proclamation should focus on the relational aspect of life. Just as the shepherd's life is determined by the will of the Father, so the life of the flock is determined by the relation to the shepherd. The focus of the passage is not on the shepherd as the constant defender of the flock, but on the willingness of the shepherd to die for the flock. That transcends all boundaries. The church is called to trust the shepherd and live as the one flock.

SECOND LESSON

The very short second lesson, 1 John 3:1–2, puts the Gospel into an eschatological framework, though it does not use the imagery of shepherd and sheep, but that of being God's children. The lectionary omits 1 John 2:28–29, which makes an appeal to remain in Christ in the present in order to have confidence *(parrhēsia)* at the Parousia (2:28; the pun in Greek is intentional). The text gives the basis for that boldness and confidence in the fact that we have become children of God through Jesus. And a new image is used, that of seeing. God is called "just" in 1:9; Jesus is named "righteous" in 2:1, 29. In 2:29, the person who does righteousness is born of God. The principle on which 3:1–2 is based is thus implied. What the Father is, the Son is; what the Son is is also characteristic of the Christian. Therefore, to do justice (righteousness) is to show you are in the logical chain of similarity and therefore child of God.

On that basis the text expresses the full confidence in the future (the *parrhēsia* of 2:28) that the title "children of God" implies. The title is a measure of the magnitude of God's love. We have the gift of being called his children, which "we are" (2:1). The idea of Christians as God's offspring appears here in the book for the first time. It is realistically conceived, as the reference to God's seed in us shows (3:9). It becomes a key motif in chap. 5.

It has a long history. Israel was God's son (Exod. 4:22; Hos. 11:1). The davidic king is given the title, too (2 Sam. 7:14; Ps. 2:7). The title argues for a special relationship between God and the child. There is a close parallel to 1 John 2 in a saying credited to R. Akiba: "Beloved are Israel because they are called sons of God. Greater love was demonstrated to them in that they were called sons of God, as it is said: 'Sons you are to the Lord your God' " (Deut. 14:1; citation from *Mishnah, Pirke Aboth* 3.18).

Such a title proves divisive. Because of it, the world "does not recognize us, because it did not recognize him." The division is not caused by elitism, but by commitment to the Son. There is a similar division between the Sons of Darkness and the Sons of Light at Qumran (1QS.III.22).

But the title also helps the Christian face the future with confidence. 1 John 3:2 makes clear how. The translation of the RSV needs to be emended on the basis of a different analysis of the original text. "Beloved, now we are God's children, and he has not yet been revealed. What we shall be, we know; because, if he is revealed, we shall be like him, for we shall see him, just as he is." The translation repunctuates the verse and identifies the subject of "reveal" as personal rather than impersonal. The analysis is based on the principle of similarity stated in connection with 2:29. In the present, Christians are confident they are God's children, since that is the name given to them. It is a reality, too, because of the hostility between Christians and the world. Christ's Parousia, referred to in 2:28, lies in the future. He therefore has not yet been revealed. But the principle of likeness gives confidence (2:28) in the status of Christians in the future. We will see him for what he really is, the glorified Son. And we will be like him. When read in conjunction with the Gospel from John 10, we state that what Jesus really is like is shown us in the good shepherd. His care for us gives us confidence in the future that ultimately lies before all people. He gathers his flock from all folds into one. And that gathering will take place. Thus the Christian looks forward confidently.

FIRST LESSON

The first lesson, Acts 4:23–33, fixes our gaze on the life of Christians in the present. It follows immediately on the trial that was the lesson for Easter III. It shows us the reaction of the Christian community to its first experience of pressure, threat, and opposition. It is a lively illustration showing the hatred of the world (1 John 3:1) and the actions of the wolves (John 10:12) toward the shepherd's flock. Peter and John, when released, return immediately to their own (4:23), that is, to the church, and report all that the council said to them. Luke assumes that the community was gathered while the two disciples were under arrest. In the background of the public trial shimmers the communal prayer of the church. The immediate unified (*homothyma-don,* 4:24) response is prayer. (Luke does not ask how an assembled group can pray such a long prayer in response to this situation without preparation; or he assumes that the Spirit guides the prayer, contained in 4:24b–30.)

The prayer falls into four sections. The address in v. 24b appeals to God under the title *despotēs* (elsewhere in the NT in Luke 2:29; 2 Pet. 2:1; Jude 4; Rev. 6:10). It is the oriental title for a supreme ruler, found some twenty-five times in the Greek Old Testament. It is immediately defined by Old Testament allusions that ascribe to him the creation of the universe (cf. the prayer of Hezekiah in Isa. 37:16–20; Neh. 9:6, etc.). This is followed in 4:25–26 by the citation of Ps. 2:1–2, ascribed to David inspired by the Holy Spirit. The text is understood messianically to apply to Jesus because of the mention of "the anointed." Vv. 27–28 apply the text to Jesus in an act of memory, which stresses that God was in control of Jesus' passion, even though the rulers and the people set themselves against Jesus. The fourth section of the prayer (4:29–30) turns to the situation of threat. It asks God for two things: to make the Christians bold in proclaiming the Gospel and to confirm it with more miracles in the name of Jesus. The earthquake that follows is in the ancient world a sign of answered prayer (cf. Exod. 19:18; Isa. 6:4, Luke 21:11; Acts 16:26). The Holy Spirit inspired them with the same kind of boldness Peter had shown in addressing the council (4:13).

What does one do in the face of opposition to the proclamation of the word? Pray—pray not that the opposition be removed, but that the church be bold in proclamation. The early church did not feel that opposition removed it from the care of God (cf. the certainty of the lesson from 1 John). The application to the church in our age at first appears obvious—until one asks why proclamation today raises so little opposition. Our prayer for boldness is needed too, not in the face of opposition from without, but apathy from within the Christian community.

The Fifth Sunday of Easter

Lutheran	Roman Catholic	Episcopal	Pres/UCC/Chr	Meth/COCU
Acts 8:26–40	Acts 9:26–31	Acts 8.26–40 or Deut. 4:32–40	Acts 9:26–31	Acts 8:26–40 or Acts 9:25–31 or Deut. 4:32–40
1 John 3:18–24	1 John 3:18–24	1 John 3:(14–17) 18–24 or Acts 8:26–40	1 John 3:18–24	1 John 3:18–24
John 15:1–8	John 15:1–8	John 14:15–21	John 15:1–8	John 15:1–8

This Sunday is the first of three to take their Gospels from the farewell discourses of the Johannine Jesus (John 13:31—17:26). The farewell discourse is a well-known literary form. Jacob (Genesis 48—49), Moses (Deuteronomy), Joshua (Joshua 23—24), David (1 Chronicles 28—29), and Paul (Acts 20:18–35) all speak them. Farewell discourses announce the speaker's impending death, give

comfort and encouragement in the face of the loss, warn against future
disunity, reveal something of the future, bless the hearers, and speak a
concluding prayer. All of these elements are included in Jesus'
farewell discourse.

GOSPEL

John 15:1–8 is the first half of a major unit in this discourse (15:9–17
is the Easter VI Gospel). It uses the metaphor of the vine and its
branches to stress the necessity to stay in unity with Jesus to avoid the
dangers of the future. The picture of the vineyard is well-known from
the Old Testament as a symbol for Israel (cf. Hos. 10:1; Ezek. 15:6;
Jer. 2:21, and above all Isa. 5:1–7). The Synoptic Gospels use the
picture eschatologically to condemn unbelieving Israel (Matt. 21:33–
44 par.). John makes two striking modifications in the tradition: (1)
Contrary to the Old Testament and the Synoptics John interprets the
vineyard figure to apply to ongoing life, not to apocalyptic judgment.
(2) The vine is no longer Israel, but Jesus and his disciples. Today's
lesson is an exhortation to constancy of faith—to ''abide in me'' (John
15:4).

John is often difficult to interpret precisely. His language moves in
circular, rather than logical, fashion. John 15:1–5 is divided into two
sections by the repeated ''I am the vine'' (15:1, 5). The first presents
the picture. God is the owner-caretaker, Christ the authentic vine, as
he is the authentic light (1:9) and bread (6:32). 15:2 is a warning: non-
bearing branches are cut off. Every branch that bears fruit is pruned
(the Greek term is ''purified'') to make it produce more fruit. There is
no description of what the pruning stands for: persecution, temptation, responsibility, and so on. Instead v. 3 goes on to offer comfort in
the face of the threat. It plays on the word *katharizō*, used in the sense
of ''prune'' in v. 2 and now in the sense ''purify.'' The pruning/purifi-
cation has taken place by the word spoken by Jesus (15:3). The
disciple is thus directed outside himself for the comfort needed. At the
same time, the pruning/purification motif in the two verses stresses
that discipleship is not a plateau of life at which one rests. Rather
Christian life is life under the constant, even growing demand to bear
fruit. It therefore has no self-security, but must be directed outside
itself, just as a branch cannot exist apart from the stock of the vine.
Therefore 15:4 ends with the command ''Abide in me.'' Christian life
is a cooperative venture. Only in Christ is fruit bearing possible.

Section 2 (15:5–8) shows how to stay in the vine. It opens in v. 5 by stating v. 4 again, but in the form of a promise. And one can rest in a promise. The alternative (15:6) is destruction, though fire is not here automatically an eschatological motif. Remaining in Christ is also a source of power, for when one is in the vine, and the words of Jesus are in the Christian ("words" here = "word" in v. 3 = "I" in v. 5), then one can pray in confidence that prayer is answered (15:7). Thus 15:5–7 shows how the command of 15:4 is at the same time resource and empowerment. Prayer is itself one of the fruits of being in the vine; therefore it is at the same time an act of glorifying the Father (15:8). Such glorification is mentioned earlier in the Gospel (cf. 12:28; 13:31; 14:13; 17:4). It takes place by being a disciple, for that shows that the Father's will in the Son is being carried out. Thus fruit bearing in John is the equivalent of belief in Paul's writings. Both lead inextricably to action that demonstrates the reality of discipleship.

SECOND LESSON

1 John 3:18–24, the second lesson, reinforces the Gospel by presenting many of the same motifs in a different configuration and to a slightly different end: the basis of confidence lies in response to the world. It begins with 3:18, a verse that should be regarded as the beginning of a new paragraph because of the "little children" at its head. It calls for a love that is not only verbally affirmed, but actually practiced (a hendiadys in "in deed and in truth"). Practical love has a practical consequence also for the lover! "By this" in 3:19 refers back to this practical love as the basis for confidence. It is a form of exterior demonstration that the word (here called "truth") is the matrix out of which one is living. By practical love we "can persuade ourselves" even before God ("him" in 3:19). Thus while the Gospel urges disciples to remain in Christ to be able to bear fruit, the Epistle argues that practical love shows that one is indeed living out of fellowship with the Son.

3:20 adds a second ground for confidence. Practical love also is the basis for knowing that God is the power in the universe. He is greater than our hearts, knows all things, and thus, when we stand self-accused and self-condemned, he overrides our hearts. Love conquers condemnation; on the basis of public, practical love, God knows what we really are. John is not urging self-interest as a reason to practice love. Then it would not be love at all. But love practiced surprises us with the accepting power of God.

The Gospel urges that remaining in Christ produces fruit in the form of prayer (15:7). 1 John again reverses the argument to affirm that boldness (*parrhēsia,* cf. 2:28) in prayer is the result of "keeping his commandments and producing the things that are pleasing before him" (3:21–22). Boldness in prayer arises from practical love. Our ongoing daily prayer-life is itself a demonstration that our hearts do not condemn us (2:21). There is no demand that this prayer must be intercessory, though the context of active love strongly implies it. The promise with the boldness is breathtakingly absolute: "We receive from him whatever we ask." It is a mark of absolute confidence.

The last short paragraph (3:23–24) defines the commandments of 3:22 as a single command with a double form of observance. The command is both to believe and to act in love (3:23). The two are not identical, but inseparable in the reality 1 John urges. Belief in his son Jesus Christ includes believing that Jesus' humanity is the place in which God's word was spoken (cf. 4:2, 15). The basis for love is not a feeling, an emotion, or an idea, but the acting out of love in and by Jesus (3:16) that impels us to the love he demands. Such love is the mode of remaining in fellowship with him ("remains in him," 3:24). But here 1 John makes a significant addition to the Gospel. There is a basis for knowing that we are in him, the Spirit. He is named here for the first time in 1 John. The significance of that naming will become clear in the next two Sundays.

The two Johannine lessons provide the occasion to address the question of the practical nature of Christian faith and life. Faith acts, says John. If it does not, then there is no relation to the Son or God. Action that is love to another is the proof that the word is working in the Christian; faith is thus not self-authenticating. But it is authentic when it acts in love. That produces confidence in prayer and when arraigned before one's accusing self.

FIRST LESSON

The first lesson (Acts 8:26–40) moves in quite a different direction. After the hearing before the council Luke records the story of Ananias and Sapphira (4:32—5:11), then recounts the second arrest by the religious authorities, this time of the apostles (5:18, presumably all twelve), their miraculous release, appearance before the council (with Gamaliel giving sage advice, 5:35–39), whipping, and warning to stop their witness. The election of the seven to serve tables and the arrest, trial, and mob murder of Stephen (6:1—7:60) led to a general persecution in which all are scattered from Jerusalem except the apostles (8:1–3). Philip, one of the seven, plays a significant role in what follows: he is the first to preach in Samaria (8:4–13; cf. 1:8); his success there leads to a visitation from Jerusalem by Peter and John (8:14–25) that led to the gift of the Holy Spirit through their hands and the condemnation of Simon Magus. Philip's activity in Samaria confirms the fact that persecution does not inhibit the plan of God, but helps it move forward (cf. 8:4). The familiar story of Philip and the Ethiopian eunuch is the second stage in that demonstration. Philip first proclaimed the word to Samaria. Now he is the first to preach the word to a non-Jew! (There is debate about the eunuch's race; Acts nowhere says he is Jewish or gentile. But the proper name "Ethiopian" in 8:27 argues against Jewishness.) The significance of this narrative is underscored in two striking ways. (1) Philip goes toward Gaza (the border city just before the desert) because an angel of the Lord directs him to do so. (The angel is really God himself, as 5:19 and 7:30 show.) Divine direction takes him to (2) a eunuch. By Old Testament law the eunuch was excluded from Israel (Deut. 23:1; Lev. 21:17–21), though there was eschatological hope (Isa. 56:3–5). The man was doubly excluded: foreigner and eunuch.

The Spirit directed Philip to join the eunuch as he read Isaiah 53 in his chariot. When the eunuch confessed he needed an exegete to help him understand Isa. 53:7–8, Philip began with that text to tell him "the good news of Jesus" (8:35). Isaiah 53 stresses the road of Jesus through humiliation to exaltation; early Christians read it as a text speaking directly of Jesus. Such a pattern of vindication by God is the basis for preaching forgiveness (Acts 5:30–31; Luke 24:46–47).

The eunuch took the initiative. He had invited Philip into the chariot to interpret Isaiah (8:31); now he asks "What is to prevent my being baptized?" (8:36). (Some see a reflection of an early Christian baptismal liturgy in this question. The interpretation is possible, but not compelling.) The question and its response show that all obstacles have been set aside. Neither race nor mutilation (the Jewish understanding of emasculation) can separate him from God any longer. What III Isaiah foresaw as an eschatological possibility is now a historical reality. Luke places into the life of the church already the realization of hope. That is the theme that comes out of this text for proclamation. And this happened by divine directive through the agency of one of those "Greek-speaking" Jews whose widows were being overlooked. God used Philip to expand the definition of the Christian community.

The Sixth Sunday of Easter

Lutheran	Roman Catholic	Episcopal	Pres/UCC/Chr	Meth/COCU
Acts 11:19–30	Acts 10:25–26, 34–35, 44–48	Acts 11:19–30 or Isa. 45:11– 13, 18–19	Acts 10:34–48	Acts 11:19–30 or Isa. 45:11– 13, 18–19
1 John 4:1–11	1 John 4:7–10	1 John 4:7–21 or Acts 11:19–30	1 John 4:1–7	1 John 4:1–11
John 15:9–17	John 15:9–17	John 15:9–17	John 15:9–17	John 15:9–17

GOSPEL

The Gospel for Easter VII, John 15:9–17, is the direct continuation of the Gospel for Easter V. That Gospel has made the point that one must stay in unity with Jesus in order to bear fruit. The disciple is not independent, self-reliant, or self-authenticating. Today's Gospel makes last Sunday's more precise. The first verses (15:9–11) make clear that to remain in Jesus means to love. The command of 15:4, "Remain in me," now becomes "Remain in my love" (15:9). Love is what characterizes the close relation of the Father to Jesus. That love became the model and the standard for his love for the disciples. That love can be uncompromising in its demands. It sent the Son into the world to save it (3:16). But it is also therefore the impelling power for the disciples' manifestation of the Son in the world (cf. 14:21). The glory of the Son would never have been made clear but for love (cf. 1:14; 2:11), and that manifestation called forth faith.

Just as the Son's history was determined by the Father's love, so the disciples' life in the world is determined by the Son's love. It calls for obedience to his commands (15:10). Here too the Son is not imposing something novel. His entire course in the world was to keep his Father's commands and to stay in his Father's love. It has been stated often, but cannot be stated too often or too forcefully in American culture: Love here is not an emotion; it is not sentimentality; it is not the warm fuzzies in the stomach. Rather love in John is always a moral force that expresses itself in obedience to the will of the Father. Thus

Jesus "did nothing on his own authority" (John 8:28); he did not seek his own will, but "the will of him who sent me" (John 5:30). That obedience in love gave him both his power and authority, and his union with the Father. So too his disciples remain in unity with him as they are obedient to his commandments of love. That obedience to him is not onerous, but is commanded "that their joy may be full" (15:11) because his joy is in them. Joy is here almost a synonym for obedience.

The next six verses expand the command to love. One might suppose that the mode of remaining in fellowship with the Son would be to love him. But 15:12 makes clear that the command is to "love one another" as Christ loved them. Thus love is also no form of mystical union or absorption into God. Love is expressed in physical acts, in sharing pain, as Christ did. V. 13 expresses it in terms of the ultimate act of love: laying down one's life for one's friends. The verse sounds proverbial, as though Jesus is citing a well-known saying. It is interpreted in 15:14–15. Friendship is a mutual relationship. Jesus' death, an expression of love, made them his *philoi*, his "loved ones." The term is properly used of the affectionate tie that holds people together. Such ties of personal interrelationship make community. R. Hillel said, "Be of the disciples of Aaron, loving peace and pursuing it, loving mankind and bringing them close to the law" (*Mishnah, Pirke Aboth* I.12; cf. Lev. 19:18). Friendship also brings an obligation: "You are my friends if you do what I command you." Jesus now calls them friends, not slaves. His presence means a new status for the disciples. Slaves are not given an insight into the plans and will of their master. Slaves obey blindly. The disciples are "friends" because they have received the full revelation that the Father gave to the Son. That revelation included the love that the Father willed the Son to show the world. They are his friends because they have heard his proclamation and recognized in him "words of eternal life" (John 6:68). That revelation also divided humankind into those who followed and those who went away (John 6:66); those who heard the revelation, "who received him, who believed in his name" (John 1:12) are his friends (15:15).

Thus the status of friend does not come from personal liking for Jesus. He has chosen them, not they him (15:16). They were chosen before they were commanded to love. They did not elect discipleship, they were called. But election is not election to eternal physical togetherness. Jesus is leaving (16:5). He called them to bear eternal fruit. Election is to mutual loving service, the mode of discipleship in the absence of Jesus. The farewell discourse prepares the disciples to continue the pattern of love initiated by the Father through the Son.

SECOND LESSON

1 John 4:1–11 is the direct continuation of last Sunday's second lesson. It divides into two unrelated and disparate sections. The first, 4:1–6, discusses how to recognize false teaching, even though it is "spirit-originated." The second, 4:7–11, is a pastiche of ideas formed into a hymnic passage on the obligation to love. Its content attaches closely to the Gospel for this day and can be used to enrich it. It repeats the themes of mutual love derived from our being born of God (4:7), of God taking the initiative in loving us (4:10), and of the death of Jesus as the great act and example of love (4:9). On that basis it urges the hearers to love one another as God loved us (4:11). The material reinforces the Gospel by adding a few other traditional motifs (life, propitiation for sins). But it does not add much to what John 15 already says.

The first six verses, however, introduce a motif into the Easter season that we have not met before in Series B. 1 John 3:24 states that the gift of the Spirit is one means of knowing that Christians are abiding in Christ and in love. 1 John 4:1, however, points out that not all spirits are the Spirit of God and calls for the testing of the spirits. These six verses are dominated by dualistic language that has its original home, biblically speaking, in apocalyptic. On the one side are the false prophets (4:1), the spirit of antichrist (4:3), the world (4:1, 3, 4, 5), and the spirit of error (4:6). On the other is the Spirit of God (4:2), the true confession (4:2), the Christian community (those "from God," 4:4, 6), and the spirit of truth (4:6). The disciple community is caught between these two opposing forces.

1 John deals with them in an interesting fashion. First of all, he has removed them from the end time into the present. (2 Thess. 2:1–10 and Revelation see the antichrist as a phenomenon of the great tribulation just before the end.) He places all of history under this apocalyptic schema, that is, he historicizes the apocalyptic.

Second, he proposes a test to determine which side any given prophet or Christian is on. The test is simple, the basic confession "Jesus Christ has come in the flesh" (4:2). A confession *(homologia)* is a short statement that formulates the fundamental tie that binds a religious community together. 1 John insists the physical, human Jesus is the Messiah, not some spirit that inhabited him at the baptism and did not die. More is at stake here than just an adequate

Christology—important as that is. 1 John ties all of the church's life to the living out of the love that was shown in Jesus' life. It is based in his real death, which removes sin and opens up access to God. Both soteriology and ethics are involved in the creed for John.

Third, 1 John argues that those who belong to God can be identified in this way because a principle well known and used in the Greek world applies: like is known by like (cf. 1 Cor. 2:10–13). People who are of God will listen to John and his like because they are of God (4:6). Thus the confession of Jesus is supplemented by this principle. The proclamation value in these verses lies in the call to use a true criterion of God's truth—Christology as it works its way out in human life and confession.

FIRST LESSON

Acts 11:19–30 is that unusual phenomenon in the New Testament, a success story. Its major point is completely unrelated to the other two lessons for the day and it marks a major step forward in the life of the church. Acts 9:1–31 make clear that Paul was called to witness to the Gentiles. Acts 9:32—11:18 tell the story of Peter's visits to Aeneas (a pagan name, 9:32–35), Tabitha (Dorcas, 9:36–42), and Cornelius (10:1–48), and the subsequent Jerusalem inquiry into this proclamation to Gentiles (11:1–18). Peter justified this unusual act by referring to the validation given by the gift of the Spirit. But proclamation to Gentiles was at best spasmodic and exceptional.

Acts 11:19–30 records the decisive (and later divisive) step forward. Four scenes tell us of the initiation and character of the first (largely?) gentile church. Acts 11:19–21 reports that unnamed Jewish Christians from Cyprus and Cyrene were converted as a result of the dispersion of Christians after the death of Stephen (11:19; cf. 8:4). These Hellenized Jewish Christians preached the Lord Jesus to Gentiles in Antioch. ("Lord" as a title would mean "world ruler" to Greeks; "Christ" would have little sense.) God blessed them ("hand of the Lord," 11:21; cf. 10:38). A "great number" turned to the Lord in faith (11:21). No mention is made either of circumcision or baptism. These Hellenized Jews did not demand conformity to Jewish law by Gentiles.

Scene 2 (11:22–24): Barnabas is sent from Jerusalem to check out this unusual action. He is the first nonapostlic emissary (cf. 8:14), himself a Cypriote and a Levite (4:36). He sees the action of God in what happens (11:23) and rejoices. He urges fidelity to the Lord, but (so far as Acts reports) also makes no demands for observance of the law or ritual purity, unusual for a Levite (11:23). (Luke calls him a "good man," the only one in Acts to get this very Greek approval!) He is also filled with Holy Spirit. Scene 3 (11:25–26): Barnabas gets Saul from Tarsus. There is no suggestion Saul has been a missionary (contrary to Gal. 1:16ff.). For a year Barnabas and Saul are active in the church (the term is used of this gentile community in 11:26 for the first time; it marks them as a Christian community equal to Jerusalem). And for the first time disciples (applied to gentile Christians! 11:25) are called Christians, the name they will bear in perpetuity.

Scene 4: When a famine is predicted by a prophet, the gentile community takes thought for the Jerusalem Christians (11:27–30). Church unity is maintained.

There are many proclamatory values in this story. Unnamed, unsung, common Christians begin the church that will commission Paul as missionary in Acts. Common run-of-the-mill Christians have significant effect. The church becomes multinational and multicultural in an unplanned way. But a man filled with Holy Spirit approves. In this case unplanned is divine plan. Barnabas affirms variety that is faithful to the Lord. And that fidelity takes seriously the unity of the church in variety by the collection for the famine-oppressed in Jerusalem.

The Ascension of Our Lord

Lutheran	Roman Catholic	Episcopal	Pres/UCC/Chr	Meth/COCU
Acts 1:1–11	Acts 1:1–11	Acts 1:1–11 or Ezek. 1:3–5a, 15–22, 26–28	Acts 1:1–11	Acts 1:1–11 or Ezek. 1:3–5a, 15–22, 26–28
Eph. 1:16–23	Eph. 1:17–23	Eph. 1:15–23 or Acts 1:1–11	Eph. 1:16–23	Eph. 1:15–23
Luke 24:44–53	Mark 16:15–20	Luke 24:49–53 or Mark 16:9–15, 19–20	Luke 28:44–53	Mark 16:9–20 or Luke 24:44–53

If it were not for Luke, we would celebrate the ascension of Jesus as part of Easter. Luke alone presents the ascension as a separate event.

He does so twice, in Acts 1:1–11 at some length and in Luke 24:50–51(53). The two accounts have much in common, but also offer significant variations and serve quite different literary functions. As the only incident to be presented in both of Luke's scrolls, the account in Acts must also have a kind of resumptive function to remind the hearers of how the first scroll ended and to impel them into the story just beginning.

It is economical to take both accounts together. The parallels and contrasts will be especially illuminating. Recall what was said in the Gospel for Easter evening (Luke 24:13–49). The first section of the Ascension Gospel is the fourth section of the long Emmaus-Jerusalem narrative discussed there. Jerusalem is elevated as *the* place where Jesus appears to his disciples and where the church has its beginning. Jesus' resurrection has vindicated him as God's Messiah. In that sense his resurrection is also his triumph. The function of this last great sequence in the Gospel is to show how Jesus enables faith in him—through his teaching about himself drawn from the Old Testament (argument from prophecy) and through the table fellowship.

GOSPEL

The Ascension Gospel (Luke 24:44–53) repeats vv. 44–49 from Easter evening. The reason for inclusion is immediately apparent: they prepare for Pentecost, since the risen Christ here tells the disciples that they will be witnesses to his resurrection and the proclamation of repentance unto forgiveness for all nations. But they are to wait in Jerusalem for the promise of the Father, for the putting on or power from on high (24:47–49). In the Gospel these words are the preliminary to the ascension.

The ascension itself is briefly, but strikingly, told. It takes place on Easter evening, at Bethany. Bethany had been identified at 19:29 as "at the Mount that is called Olivet." Here Jesus had made preparations for his entry into Jerusalem. Now he leaves (parted, *diestē*, v. 51) from the same place. (The verb *diestē* is itself a kind of repetition of the verb "stood," *estē*, in v. 36; it forms an inclusion around the passage.) The Mount of Olives played a major role in Jewish Messianic expectation, being the place where the Messiah was expected to come before he entered Jerusalem (cf. Zech. 14:3–11 to Jesus' words in Matt. 21:21–22). Jesus, the vindicated Christ, *leaves* from there.

He leaves in the act of blessing. The upraised hands are the proper posture for blessing (cf. Lev. 9:22; Sir. 50:20). The blessing is probably the blessing from Num. 6:22–27; "So shall you put my name upon the people of Israel, and I will bless them.'' The last great act of Jesus is a priestly act; the final Christophany is that of the priest who leaves his people with the name of God, who will bless them with his promise and power from on high (Luke 24:49). His leaving does not leave them bereft, for the blessing assures them that God is with them. (There may be a quiet polemic against John the Baptist in this narrative. John, according to Luke 1:5, was born of parents who were both of priestly stock. Yet his father could not pronounce the blessing [Luke 1:22]. Acts 19:3 suggests that there was a group among Luke's readers who revered John the Baptist. They may, like the Qumran community, have thought of a priestly messiah who took precedence over the King Messiah. But Luke has taken pains to show that John is inferior to Jesus in every respect, as the angelic words of Zechariah and Mary in chap. 1 suggest. The infant John in his mother's womb does obeisance to the unborn Jesus [Luke 1:44], and John is put in jail before Jesus is even baptized [Luke 3:18–20]. Jesus, not John, is the end-time priest in Luke.)

The reaction of the disciples shows their faith. They prostrate themselves face down upon the ground (Luke 24:52, *proskynēsantes autō*). So too in Sir. 50:21–24. The final scene in Luke is not a separation scene. There is no sorrow, no tears; but joy accompanies the disciples as they return to Jerusalem. Jesus' departure is at the same time his exaltation to heaven and the disciples' commissioning. They go to Jerusalem (24:52) and, as in Sir. 50:24, are "constantly in the temple blessing God." (The verb used of their praise of God is the same used of Jesus blessing them.)

FIRST LESSON

Acts 1:1–11 is the other Lukan account of the ascension. It opens up the Book of Acts. Whereas in Luke the ascension is the fitting conclusion to the narrative about Jesus, here his leaving is the prelude that fits the disciples for their work of witness to him. The striking variations from Luke 24 all tend to that end. The narrative falls into three sections (four if one reads through v. 14, where the fitting narrative break comes):

1:1–5	Historical resume of Jesus and the apostles from a later vantage point.
1:6–8	Clarification of the nature of the royal rule of Christ. Not politics, but witness.

1:9–11   The actual ascension narrative.
1:12–14   The return to the city and activity there.

The narrative has a number of functions. First of all, it bridges the gap between the resurrection of Jesus and the beginning of the church. The vantage point from which Luke writes is third-generation Christianity (cf. Luke 1:1–4). Jesus and the apostles are figures of the past. Jesus' life (Luke 1—24) is what he began to do and teach. What the disciples do and teach is what Jesus does and teaches after his ascension (1:1). The tie is made through the commandment he gave *and* through the teaching he did "for forty days" (1:3). The number is a striking variation from the chronology of Easter Day in Luke 24. The chronologies are irreconcilable. They serve different functions. In the Gospel the immediate ascension ratifies the commission with immediate blessing. In Acts 1 the forty days are the proper time for full and complete teaching to take place (cf. the number forty in Exod. 24:18; Deut. 9:9; 1 Kings 19:8; Luke 4:2; 2 Esd. 14:42–44; 2 Baruch 76). A much later rabbinic tradition suggests that teaching and learning something forty times makes the student a competent teacher. Jesus' teaching about the "kingdom of God" is the teaching of the resurrected Christ, given by the Holy Spirit (1:2). Thus the disciples, properly outfitted, continue the teaching of Jesus. After forty days Jesus could leave, because his teaching was clear.

Acts 1:5–8 is significant because it removes the disciples from the political arena of the Roman empire. The power the disciples get is not political, but pneumatic. (This point is made throughout Acts, whenever Christians confront Roman authorities.) The church is no threat to Rome, which was in the first century suspicious of all associations, for political reasons. The disciples are not even to engage in apocalyptic speculations (Acts 1:7). For Luke, the Holy Spirit is the power that impels the church into witness, a witness that embraces the entire known world, from Jerusalem through hated Samaria to Rome, the "end of the earth" (cf. in Ps. Sol. 8:15). The church is directed to a future that Luke knows stretches out for a distance before it. In that long future the church needs a sense of continuity with its Lord and its origins. Both are given through the forty days that lead to the ascension and the subsequent gift of the Spirit of Pentecost.

The actual ascension is realistically portrayed, as it is not in Luke 24. Jesus moves to heaven via the medium of a cloud (cf. Dan. 7:13,

14). His ascension is also his enthronement as the exalted Son of man.
The apostles watch the event unroll before their eyes. It is clear that
Jesus is absent in a way he was not before the ascension; that fact is
underscored by the words of the two men (angels, as in Luke 24:4).
They give no interpretation of his leaving, stating merely that he
would return in the same way (time not specified, cf. Acts 1:7). Thus
the ascension puts the disciples into the situation of the church
throughout history: living in the memory and witness of the resurrected Christ while witnessing to him in the promise of his return.
The paragraph that is not included in the lectionary (Acts 1:12–14)
stresses that fact. The disciples return to the upper room. The eleven
names are listed (thus preparing for the election of Matthias in vv.
15–26) of the disciples who had been faithful to Jesus (cf. Luke
6:13–16). To them is added mention of the women who had served him
(Luke 8:1–3) and his mother and brothers (cf. Luke 8:19–21). There is
no suggestion in Luke that his family thought him demented (as in
Mark 3:21), nor does Luke record that all fled in the garden of
Gethsemane (as in Mark 14:50). They had all been at the cross (Luke
23:49), sharing his death. They are in Luke the faithful who wait for
the Spirit in prayer.

The ascension in Acts is thus in actuality more a narrative about the
church and its task (witness to the present significance of the risen
Christ) than it is a christological statement. Proclamation will stress
that the church is still in exactly the same position in history, with the
same message and the same assignment. The ascension is anything but
a report of a past event. It leads to the account of Acts, an account that
is open-ended.

SECOND LESSON

The second lesson, Eph. 1:16–23, is a complement to the Lukan
ascension. The writer of Ephesians, a Jewish-Christian disciple of
Paul, writes the letter somewhere between A.D. 80 and 100, a period in
which the gentile majority in the church is beginning to disregard or
write off the Jewish Christians. Ephesians is a magnificent appeal to
realize the true character of the one universal church by refusing to
allow separatist walls to divide (2:14–15). The appeal is based upon
the relation of the one church to its enthroned Lord, who rules in the
world through the church. The letter is written with a grandeur and
largesse of style that is almost impossible to reproduce in English.
Long sentences, with the heaping up of synonymous nouns in geniti-
val chains, dependent clauses tumbling one upon another, vocabulary

unusual and exotic, and all used in the service of a concept that matches the grandeur of the language. Small wonder that Ephesians (along with John 17) has dominated the ecclesiological thinking of theologians and been the charter of the ecumenical movement. Chap. 1 of Ephesians is made up of two long sentences. Scholars find evidence for the use of cultic, liturgical language in each. The first (1:3–14) is a long *berachah* (i.e., blessing) on God. (2 Cor. 1:3–7 and 1 Pet. 1:3–5 are the only New Testament parallels.) It is a Jewish liturgical form (cf. the Psalms of Thanksgiving at Qumran). The *berachah* blesses God for his plan for the church, worked out before the universe was made (1:4). That plan was a mystery whose meaning is made clear only in Christ (1:9–10), the cosmic Ruler from whom the church has its understanding of election (1:4), redemption (1:7), sonship (1:5), knowledge (1:9f.), the Spirit (1:13), and its unity ("sum up all things in Christ," 1:10).

Our lesson is the second sentence of the chapter, a long prayer of thanksgiving and intercession (1:15–23). This prayer is significant at ascensiontide because it correlates all that the writer prays for the church with the risen and enthroned Christ. He is described in 1:20 as the fulfillment of Ps. 110:1 ("and seated him at his right hand in the super-heavenlies"). His resurrection is also enthronement, and that enthronement is cosmic. There is no power that is not subject to him, whether heavenly or earthly ("rule, authority, power, lordship," 1:21, are all titles for cosmic, heavenly deities; cf. Col. 1:16; Eph. 2:2). He is seated in the "super-heavenlies," that is, in the realm of God that is over the seven heavens that are above the earth. These seven heavens are the place where the "seven governors" rule, from which they control all the world. They are the sun, moon, and the five planets known to the ancient peoples of the eastern Mediterranean. The whole system is well described in *Corp. Herm.* 1.9. The term "super-heavenlies" is characteristic of Ephesians (1:3, 20; 2:6; 3:10; 6:12). The cosmic Christ is opposed by cosmic evil; but the resurrection shows that all these powers are subject to him, are under his feet (Ps. 8:6 cited in Eph. 1:22); therefore he must be in the super-heavenlies.

Ephesians thus bases its vision of the church on the confession that God raised Jesus from the dead (cf. Rom. 10:9; Acts 2:32 for similar creedal statements). His Lordship over the universe also makes Jesus the "head over all things for the church, which is his body" (1:22–23). The church is the place where his rule is most evident; therefore the church must know what its hope is, its future; what its wealth is, its inheritance among the saints. The Lordship of Jesus makes the church a single, cosmic entity in which the unity he gives is to be realized (cf. 4:1-6). Thus, for the author of Ephesians, the position of the enthroned Lord determines the character, the unity, the hope, the future, and the task of the church. While Acts grounds its view of the church in the absence of the ascended Lord, Ephesians grounds it in the superior position of that Lord. The two are complementary. Ephesians provides the grandeur of language that is lacking in Acts 1:1-11.

The Seventh Sunday of Easter

Lutheran	Roman Catholic	Episcopal	Pres/UCC/Chr	Meth/COCU
Acts 1:15–26	Acts 1:15–17, 20–26	Acts 1:15–26 or Exod. 28:1–4, 9–10, 29–30	Acts 1:15–17, 21–26	Acts 1:15–26 or Exod. 28:1–4, 9–10, 29–30
1 John 4:13–21	1 John 4:11–16	1 John 5:9–15 or Acts 1:15–26	1 John 4:11–16	1 John 4:11–21
John 17:11b–19	John 17:11b–19	John 17:11b–19	John 17:11–19	John 17:11–19

FIRST LESSON

Easter VII is the Sunday between the ascension and Pentecost. That gives it some of its unusual flavor. The lesson from Acts 1:15–26 takes us back to the promise of the Spirit made to the disciples by Jesus and the directive that they wait in Jerusalem for that gift (Acts 1:4–5). Today's lesson is the one specific narrative Luke uses to fill the ten-day gap between the ascension and Pentecost. (He does give a summary statement that lists the names of the eleven together with Mary, other women, and Jesus' brothers, 1:12–14.)

The narrative is more than a filler, even though it also has that function. Acts 1:15 reports that Peter addressed the community of brothers who numbered 120. The masculine "brothers" is in this case significant, since the Mishnah contains the (later) tradition that 120 people was the minimum number for a town to establish its own small council (*Mishnah* IV.4.1.6). Luke suggests that the church was a community legally competent to have its own internal structure.

Peter's address (1:16–22) points out that God's will, revealed by the inspired David (Ps. 69:25; 109:8; v. 20), was that Judas's treachery should lead to his death and replacement (1:16, 21–22). His death, a disease that burst his entrails, was a mark of divine judgment (2 Macc. 9:7–12; Sir. 10:9). The story of his death and the naming of his field showed the public distaste for his actions. Judas was to have shared in the ministry of the Twelve (1:17).

Now his place was to be filled. A new apostle was to be elected. Two men, Joseph Barsabbas and Matthias, meet the qualifications mentioned by Peter: They must have been disciples who experienced Jesus' ministry from beginning to end (from John's baptism to the ascension, 1:22). Thus it is not scholarship, education, speaking ability, social grace, or some other personal quality that makes an apostle. After prayer that mentions apostleship (1:24–25) the selection is made by some form of lot. Ancients regarded that as a mode to insure that people not manipulate and that God's choice be clear (cf. 1 Sam. 14:41; Prov. 16:33). The lot fell on Matthias (1:26).

The apostles are in some unique fashion "witness to his resurrection" (1:22). Paul suggests the same thing in his mention of the Twelve as among the first to whom the resurrected Christ appeared (1 Cor. 15:5). The number twelve is significant, either because a council of twelve had the leadership (1:20 uses the term *episkopē,* oversight) or because they are representative of Israel (cf. Luke 22:29–30). Their role in Acts is fascinating. They appear only as a collective that stays in Jerusalem (cf. 8:1). They represent the church waiting for the Son of man in the Holy City, the center of the universe (cf. Psalm 48).

SECOND LESSON

1 John 4:13–21 gives the impression that it is made up of a number of smaller units (tracts or sermons?) that the author has used earlier. That would account for the recurrence, time and again, of the terms and motifs in several passages. Certainly this second lesson will sound familiar to the listener who has been paying even minimal attention to the lessons in this Easter cycle. This tendency to recurrent language makes proclamation difficult and/or repetitious. One needs to look for the small variations in phraseology or motif that provide the development from what has been heard before.

There are many motifs now familiar to us in this passage. A listing will make that clear. (1) The gift of the Spirit assures us that we are remaining in God and God in us (4:13; cf. 3:24). (2) The Spirit is tied to the act of confessing Jesus (4:15; cf. 4:2; 2:22–23). And this confessing

reinforces our abiding in God. There are two new variations that
come in 4:13–16. The Son is sent as "savior of the world" (4:14). That
is what we see and confess. Thus v. 14 is the corrective to v.
12 (not included in the lectionary). While no one can see God, we can see
what he has done, and that is send a Savior. The term occurs only here
and in John 4:42 in Johannine literature. (It is only in Phil. 3:20 in
Paul, but frequent in later New Testament books: 2 Tim. 1:10; Titus
1:4; 2:13, 3:6; five times in 2 Peter.) The title is frequently applied to
the benefactors of the ancient world, whether healing gods, emperors,
or lesser benefactors. Here it gives content to the confession "Son of
God" in 4:15 (cf. 2:22; the flesh is not mentioned here). The other
variation is in the phrase "we have believed his love" in 4:16. The
phrase implies that seeing that Jesus is the Savior calls us to faith in
the God who loves. Only in Jesus can we see God or know him in his
acting to save. Thus the Christology here is functional, not specula-
tive.

The last paragraph of the lesson also replicates earlier motifs: To
remain in love is to remain in God (4:16). Such love produces boldness
before God (4:17). Love is to be demonstrated in a practical way as
love to one another (4:20–21). This is founded in the priority of God's
loving (4:19). In all this there is nothing that has not been heard
before. The new in this short homily is found in defining God as love
(4:16), in specifying that the boldness is on the day of judgment, that
is, the final judgment (4:17). 2:28 speaks of the Parousia of Jesus, but
without overt mention of judgment or boldness. 3:21 speaks of boldness, but applies it to ongoing prayer. The eschatological stress here is
almost unique.

To it is tied the note that love throws fear out, if love has been
perfected (4:18). That is because fear, the antithesis of boldness,
anticipates punishment. Love that produces boldness faces the final
judgment in the confidence that we shall be children of God as he
(Jesus) is his Son. That freedom from fear produces the vital quality of
life that loves.

GOSPEL

John 17: 11b–19 is the central block in the great concluding prayer
of the farewell discourses. It sums up Johannine theology on the work
of Christ in relation to his disciples. It looks to the time when Jesus and
the disciples are no longer together. 17:1–5 asks the Father to glorify
the Son via the crucifixion. 17:6–19 is a prayer for the disciples, while
17:20–24 prays for the unity of the generations to come as they live out

their faith in the world. The prayer concludes with a summation of Jesus' work as the revealer sent to the world.

The section on the disciples opens with the affirmation that the disciples have received the revelation Jesus came to give, have kept the word he gave, and know that he came from the Father (17:6-8). They are separated out from the world; therefore Jesus prays for them. In them Jesus is glorified, because they show by their faith that he is indeed the one sent by God who has all that is the Father's (17:9-10).

Jesus' intercessions for the disciples are called forth by his imminent departure from the world. While he was in the *kosmos*, he kept and guarded his disciples, except for the "son of destruction" (17:12; the reference is clearly to Judas; cf. 2 Thess. 2:3). Once again an apocalyptic phrase is used nonapocalyptically by John. Jesus prays that the disciples may be preserved by his Father's name (i.e., power). Thus they will experience the oneness he has with the Father (17:11).

Jesus gave his disciples the word committed to him by the Father. That word has not removed them from the world (17:11), but it has put a deep gulf between them and the world, expressed in the hatred of the world (17:14). They are hated because they, like the Son, are not of the world. It is this hatred, centered in the "evil one" (17:15), that makes the prayer necessary. Jesus does not pray for some kind of ascension for all believers, nor does he ask for a mystical ascent of the soul that would remove disciples from the world. He prays rather for God to preserve them (17:15). He does that by consecrating them (17:17, *hagiason*); the term means here "set apart." They are to be dedicated to being sent by the Son, as the Son was sent by the Father (17:18). The Son's dedication meant the carrying out of the Father's will in the world; it led to his crucifixion/glorification. Disciples are dedicated to the same glorious mission (I am glorified in them, 17:10).

The setting of the last Sunday in Easter means that in the lectionary the sanctification looks toward Pentecost. Proclamation will point to the fact that the prayer of Jesus was realized and is being realized in the "sentness" of God's people today. We are not the original disciples, but the hallowing of God's people through service and witness still goes on today. People who catch the vision discover the joy of which Christ spoke and learn the care with which God accompanies his people.